Dedication

To Mom and Dad
for all your love, care and encouragement.
And especially for your support
in the writing of this book. I love you bunches!

Also to my best friend, Katrina Shaw,
who is also my first cousin (on the side)!
I luv ya, girl! You're the best!
Thanks for all you do – much of what is in this
book has been a part of our late night,
or should I say early morning talks!

And to every gal who ever reads this book.
We're driving down this lane together,
my friend, so let's get cruising!
We can be part of the Old Maid Caravan –
"God's Will or Bust!"

Life In the Single Lane

Aprill M. Brunson

Portrait of the author courtesy of Kimberlee Bloom

ISBN 0-9758614-0-9

Printed in the United States of America

Contents

Lord, save us!

We're going to drown!

Matthew 8:25 NIV®

Chapter 1

Drowning In the Sea of Un-Single

Your heart's desire has always been to be a wife and mother. While it may not be the only desire you have tucked away in your treasure chest of dreams, it is a special and important one nonetheless. Depending upon your own personal time table, it would be absolutely wonderful to just find that special man with whom you can serve God better together with than apart. The one to whom you can pledge your life to and vow to stand by his side for better or for worse. <sigh> To bear his children and raise them up in the nurture and admonition of the Lord. <double sigh> But as the days, weeks, months and years slowly go by, there is one small problem that continually plays out in your life. It is an ever-constant dilemma. You remain…single.

Okay, so maybe you're the kind of person that just loves being all alone. You think loneliness is the height of satisfaction and fulfillment. You have no one special in your life to care for or be cared for by. No one to serve the Lord with or anyone to vow anything to. You're feeling sick (you know what I mean) and are utterly and completely fine with it. Frankly, you enjoy watching all your friends you grew up with and even the young people you go to church with or work with, find the one of their dreams, fall in love, get married and then have children. Oh, you also especially relish watching those who are younger than you are tying the knot and then floating off to the Land of Marriage. Without a doubt, you take great pleasure from being left totally in the dust. You think that the smell of dirt in your face is so phenomenal. I mean, everyone should experience the sensation of grains of dirt grinding into their teeth, right!? When the preacher mentions something like, "Well, all you married people know such and such," you feel so involved and entirely on the same page.

Uh-uh, right! If you're anything like I am, these are the furthest thoughts from your mind – aforementioned thoughts don't even "think" about heading your way! You are not, in any sense of the word, this kind of person. As a matter of fact, you are quite the opposite.

You are actually drowning. And to put it simply, it's quite an amazing feat since you are not even in water. You are drowning in the Sea of Un-Single. That's right! Everywhere you turn there are, what most of those inhabiting planet earth call, "married people." But to you, the single, they're the "un-single." They have something that sets them apart and, in your mind and a lot of the time in their minds as well, something far above what you have. Something better. Something more fulfilling. Something that some think completes them more than anything a single person has. But is that really so? Is one status inferior to the other? Can you be rescued from the churning, dark waters that are choking the very life out of you? Is there such a thing as a life raft? Is it possible to be complete while still being single? Can you ever be confident in your singleness? Does God really know what He's doing?

Does God really know what He's doing?

In the pages of this book, I will share my own personal journey of how the Lord Jesus Christ has brought me to the place of accepting what He has given to me – life in the single lane. I want you to recognize the great adventure that comes from accepting that gift and how you can bless Him in return with a life of service. I am still driving in that lane. I haven't switched to the married lane and am now sharing my 20/20 hindsight vision with you. You are going to get it straight from an old maid's mouth who is in this life of singleness right along with you. I am single, unmarried, unattached with no prospect on the horizon – not even a glimmer. And in all honesty, I'm okay with being single, and however long I live like this, well, that's okay too. How can that be? Because God has a plan and is in control and without a doubt it is GOOD and it is AWESOME!

My prayer for you, as an awesome single woman of God, is that after reading this book you will be able to say with acceptance and confidence that your state of singleness is a gift from the Lord and your desire will be to use it for God's glory. I pray you will no longer feel like you're hopelessly drowning in the Sea of Un-Single, but that God's perfect plan for your life is out of this world. And where He has you serving today is exactly where you should be. There is no better place to be than in God's will. I pray that you, my dear friend, know how important, precious and uniquely special you are in the eyes of your Heavenly Father. He is excited, no *ecstatic*, about the awesome plans He has for you and desperately wants you to trust Him to carry out those plans in your life.

I want you to know that it's okay to live life in the single lane. Nothing is wrong with you if you do - in spite of the opinions of those around you who say it's close to the time or even high time for you to stop being so picky in your choice of a husband and get on the ball and settle down. It is definitely not inferior to any other lane in life. In fact, it's an exciting route to travel – believe me, I know! Around every bend in the road is another adventure, another occasion to serve, and another opportunity to experience all that God has for you. Let me assure you that the scenery is spectacular and the other motorists you'll meet along the way are some extraordinary people. Despite popular opinion, there is peace, contentment, and fulfillment in being in the single lane as a single, non-married, unattached, awesome woman who makes God the focus of her attention and serves Him with a passion. So what's the key? Keep reading and you'll hear it straight from the Old Maid's mouth! ☺

Life is God's novel.

Let him write it.

Isaac Bashevis Singer

Chapter 2

Give Me the Perfect Life

Everyone has expectations in life, and in our minds it is definitely something simple and smooth with everything in its place – a perfect life would be nice but unfortunately things in this world are far from impeccability. What we want to be when we grow up, the kind of car that we think is the absolute coolest, how many kids we want to have, our dream job, the ideal place to live, the list is endless. Before we reach that thing in life called "adulthood" we seem to think that things will go the way we've expected it to. Maybe we've never out and out said that, but in the back of our little minds, it's there and as the time approaches for it to come to pass, our anticipation is tremendous.

I am no different. Since I was a little girl, I have had one dream and expectation of what I wanted to be when I grew up and what I wanted out of life. In my little mind, there was nothing else for little Aprill to do and nothing else to consider as an option. I wanted to be a wife and mother. My own mother, bless her, has been that beautiful example of what it means to care for your family in love and that's what I wanted to do. As I grew up, I never wanted to be anything else. Oh I might have thought it would be neat to be an airline stewardess and fly to different and exciting places, but always in the back of my mind would be that dream that I expected to be a reality.

You can flip through my photo albums and find me at all different ages doing "mommy stuff." I have this picture of when I was about four years old (grinning happily, my hair in pigtails), playing "house" outside on some old boards my dad had gotten from somewhere. In my little kitchen, the cups, plates, pots and pans are placed neatly about with even a plate, cup and fork or spoon set out on the "table" for someone (who I don't remember now). My dolls are to one side, perhaps taking their nap. I suppose that all little girls are like that, since God has specifically designed women with that special something in our makeup, which makes us women. However, I think that instinct can be nurtured and developed or completely snuffed out. Are we women by God's definition or the world's? But more on that later. Back to my dream life!

Okay, because of my desire to be a wife and mother, my idea of the perfect life would be to graduate from high school and immediately thereafter get married to the man of my dreams. Such a man would be one of Godly character and integrity; full of the Holy Spirit. A man of good and honest report. A man of conviction with a vision of how to serve God with a passion. One who loves the Lord above all else. (Girls, don't be afraid to set your standards high. God is more than able to bring you a man after His own heart. Don't settle for anything less than God's best!)

Well, according to my perfect plan, the next thing on the list would be kids. When the Lord saw fit He would bless us with children - as soon and as many as was His will (I've always thought it would be so neato to have twins!). Psalm 127:3-5 says, "Behold, children are a *heritage* from the LORD, The fruit of the womb is a *reward*. Like arrows in the hand of a warrior, So are the children of one's youth. *Happy* is the man who has his quiver *full* of them; They shall not be ashamed, But shall speak with their enemies in the gate." [NIV®. Italics mine.] Next, we would raise them in the nurture and admonition of the Lord. Guiding and teaching them to serve the King of kings with everything in them, and glorify Him in all that they did. Life wouldn't all be peachy, it would have its ups and downs, but that was okay, we would handle it together and do great things for God.

I wanted to do things God's way and according to His Word. When other girls were seeking a career, I just wanted to be a homemaker. I mean, I wanted to stay home and be a Proverbs 31 Woman and a Titus 2 Woman. My aspirations in life were not terrible, awful things, they were good things! Things straight out of God's Word. Surely the Lord would grant my perfect desires and all would go well with me. That is the way it works, right?

I totally missed God's plan.

Boy was I wrong! My seemingly flawless blueprints for the life of Aprill Brunson looked so good to me, but upon closer observation there was a glitch. A BIG one! One that I didn't plan for!

God's plan. That's right! In desiring my perfect life, I totally missed God's plan. And this was not just any plan, but one that was specifically orchestrated for me and only me by the Creator of the Universe. He had this composed before He ever created the heavens and the earth. And it was *good.* But it was not just good it was awesome! However, little ol' me was so caught up with what *I* wanted, good things that they were, that I missed it entirely. I was willing to wait for God's perfect and holy timing on everything else but when to send that guy along. And you know the funny thing is without that extremely crucial component, my plan would fail miserably. And that is just what it did.

What was it that Solomon said? "The plans of the heart belong to man, But the answer of the tongue is from the LORD. All the ways of a man are clean in his own sight, But the LORD weighs the motives." (Pro. 16:1-2 NASB) That could not be truer in my life. My expectations were just that. Mine. Not God's, mine. Someone once said, "Most people wish to serve God – but only in an advisory capacity." Ouch! By planning out my little life and expecting it to come to pass, I was informing God that He needed to adjust His plans to fit mine. Now that sounds completely rational. "Um, excuse me, Lord, here are the blueprints for my life. Please note the "Marital Timeline" section, paragraph forty-two for explicit details. I would really like to stay on schedule as much as possible – preferably at all times." Y-yeah, right!

As the days of my life slipped by, the lane of "singleness" stretching endlessly before me with no exit sign in sight, it became one of those times when you learn things the hard way. The perfect life is not what I come up with, but what God has carefully written out for me. His plan is so much better than mine is anyway. And when God is at work, without question it is going to be good. So basically, tell your imperfect little plan "goodbye" and "hello!" to God's plan. Hey! You've heard it straight from the Old Maid's mouth! ☺

God is the beyond
in the midst of our lives.

Dietrich Bonhoeffer

Chapter 3

Then Comes Reality

Talk about your plans falling through! I am going on five years past graduation and still not counted among the un-single. At one point in my life, I thought that eighteen would be the perfect age for marrying – you know my plan to graduate and immediately thereafter get married? Boy were my eyes clouded! Well, as the years since being the "perfect marrying age" have ticked by and continue to in rapid succession, it becomes more and more evident that my definition of "immediately after graduation" is obviously not God's. My personally designed roadmap has an off ramp on the "Single Turnpike" that does not exist in real life. Yes, my plan has completely and utterly flopped. It hasn't just died, it is now deceased, expired, stone cold, and decaying expeditiously.

Here I am coming down on spinsterhood like a loaded freight train off the steepest mountain and I'm getting bluer by the mile. Okay, so I am only three years past twenty, not seven years until I'm thirty! (I tell my best friend, who is forty-six days older than I am and still an old maid that it is all about perspective. If we say that it is only seven years until we are thirty it can be very depressing. But! If we say that we are only three years past twenty, then it is not so bad. For some reason though, she is not impressed!) Believe me some days, a single person whose desire is to get married, feels like they are going to be single forever! (Come on, girls, let me hear your applause!!!)

Yes, the roadway before me may look gloomy, depressing, disheartening and woeful, but then comes the good part. Reality. Oh yes, that is the good part! Because "…we know that all things work together for good to them that love God, to them who are the called according to His purpose." (Rom. 8:28, KJV)

Every year that passes and with every single mile marker that flies by ("single," get it? Ha! Ha!), and there is still "no go" to my plan, I can see how imperfect and incomplete it really is, but how perfect and complete God's plan is. As pieces of the puzzle fall into place, it is easier to see how God does have a strategy and that it is a good one. Far better than anything I could ever come up with in my most extravagant imagination. The reality is that all things, even me being single, works for good. Why? Because God's plans for us are not only good and downright awesome, but also the ultimate best for us. God said it. Believe it.

Isn't that exciting!? "For since the beginning of the world men have not heard, nor perceived by the ear, neither hath the eye seen, O God, beside thee, what he hath prepared for him that waiteth for him." (Isa. 64:4, KJV) God says, "You have no idea of how good I've planned it for you. You've never *heard* of something so awesome. You've never *seen* something as spectacular as this. Wait on Me and you will be blessed."

God is awesome!

If you and I let El Elyon – The Sovereign Ruler of the Universe - be in control of our lives, it's a given that it's going to be awesome! Let God be in the driver's seat and not just a passenger! "For the LORD your God is the God of gods and the Lord of lords, the great, the mighty…." (Deut. 10:17) God is awesome, His plans are awesome and what He does in our lives when we allow Him to do His work is awesome. God will never shortchange us. He will never let us down. What He does in our lives could not be accomplished or be as awesome if He didn't do it. Believe me! It could not. "'For My thoughts are not your thoughts, Neither are your ways My ways,' declares the LORD." (Isa. 55:8)

Corrie ten Boom said, "God has no problems, only plans." That is so true! God's plan for my life and yours does not have any glitches, flaws, blemishes, imperfections or defects in it. It contains no problems even in the tiniest sense. It is immaculate in every way. It is impeccable. If He says there's an exit up ahead there will be one. There is not one part that He hasn't carefully considered and weighed in the balance to make sure it isn't wanting in any way. It is exactly the way it should be. It is God's way. Most of us want it to be our way, but "let's never forget that some of God's greatest mercies are His refusals. He says no in order that He may, in some way we cannot imagine, say yes. All His ways with us are merciful. His meaning is always love." (Elisabeth Elliot) The reality is that God loves us and would never do anything that would harm us or not be good for us. When He says no to our expectations and our plans, it is because He has something far greater than that.

God's plan is impeccably immaculate.

The reality is that His thoughts toward us are *precious* and in great abundance. (Psalm 139:17) It is amazing that God would think any thoughts, much less precious ones, about this little no body on planet earth who deserves nothing good at all.

I am a sinner who crucified God's Son with my sin. I don't deserve even a nice glance from God. But the reality is because of what His Son, Jesus Christ, did on the cross for me, I am blessed beyond measure. He only has my best and your best in mind as He leads and guides us down the path He's prepared. Wow! Now that is quite the reality! "Many are the plans in a man's heart, But the counsel of the LORD, it will stand." (Pro. 19:21)

However, there is always that "S" thing which likes to get in our way. You know, when we try to do things God's way by accepting and believing this reality that all things work together for good, the "S thing steps in when and where it's not wanted. It crashes the party on a regular basis. It has no qualms about ruining and destroying your life. It ruthlessly extracts the joy and peace right out of you. It's the roadblock of all roadblocks! It's one detour you don't want to follow! What is this "S" thing? And what in the world does it all have to do with the "C" thing (whatever that is!)? Keep reading and you'll get it straight from the Old Maid's mouth! ☺

But godliness with contentment is great gain.

1 Timothy 6:6

Chapter 4

Struggling With That "C" Thing

There was a time that if I thought about driving down the single lane for the rest of my life, I would lose it. My little brain would go on overload and it'd get very depressing. I wanted to get married so bad. There would be days when I would cry, "Lord, I am so tired of waiting! I can't stand it any longer! Please send this guy!"

Have you ever struggled and done battle with that "C" thing. I'm sure you know the one that I'm talking about. That hard-to-accomplish-but-really-really-good-for-you-thing called "Contentment." Sometimes it seems that no matter how hard you try to achieve it, it's just beyond your reach. But why does striving to become like that one word cause such trials and tribulations in our lives?

Yes, because of the biggest and baddest roadblock – that "S" thing. You know it too. It's what rears its ugly head more often than not (a big head at that), and is so notorious for producing multiple, complex and rather aggravating, annoying problems. If we could only get rid of it somehow, the world would definitely be a better place. Perhaps we could find a way to put it into exile – just ship it off to some distant desolate island somewhere and never have to worry about it again! Wouldn't that be great? Instead of the "S Roadblock," it would be the "Island of the S." But I haven't figured out exactly how to do that yet (when I do, I'll let you know!).

You guessed it. The "S" thing is none other than "Self." Self is the roadblock that stands in the way of continuing down the lane God has placed you in. When self focuses on itself, anything that crosses it ignites the fuse and all does not go well. In trying to be content we are fighting against ourselves. Self wants things done its own way and most of the time being content means accepting things differently than the way we want them. Self's desire is to send you on a wild, bumpy and good-for-nothing detour that leads you far away from God's plan. And self puts up a pretty tough fight, it will kick and scream for what it wants. Fighting against yourself is what makes it so hard to accomplish contentment.

But what does it mean exactly to be content? First of all, contentment means to trust God fully to do His perfect work in our imperfect lives in His perfect time. "Trust in the LORD with all your heart, And do not lean on your own understanding. In all your ways acknowledge Him, and He will make your paths straight." (Pro. 3:5-6) Yes, that comprises of us keeping our inept hands off of the situation entirely. Throw your personally designed, unreliable roadmap away and consult God's roadmap instead! We take our desires to Him, lay them at His feet and leave them there – and no going back and picking them up again to see if you can get things done a little better! You can't! There is no borrowing allowed!

Always consult God's accurate and totally reliable roadmap!

There's a song that Philips, Craig and Dean sing that's called "Only You" written by Randy Phillips. It says, "You are Lord all by Yourself, You reign alone upon Your throne of righteousness. Only You." That is so true! God does not need our help to do His job. I don't know that any of us actually out and out say, "Lord, I can do a better job of navigating than you can, so why don't you let me take over things from here." But by not leaving things to Him, that is exactly what we are saying. I know I should have been right there along side Job when God asked him, "Where were you when I laid the foundations of the earth? Tell Me, if you have understanding." (Job 38:4) God then goes on for sixty-eight verses straight painting a very clear picture of Who is in control – the Alpha and the Omega. "Man is like a breath; His days are like a passing shadow." (Psa. 144:4) "Certainly every man at his best state is but vapor." (Psa. 39:5b) "Shall the one who contends with the Almighty correct Him? He who rebukes God, let him answer it." (Job 40:2) Ouch! I think God can handle things without our well-intended interference, don't you? He can be trusted. Navigation down any lane for Him is a no-brainer. Meister Eckhart said, "God can do more without us than we can do without him."

"God can do more without us than we can do without him."

Contentment also means to rest in Him. "Rest in the LORD…" (Psa. 37:7) In other versions, it says to "be still before the Lord." When you are not resting, what are you doing? Yes, rushing about trying to make things happen. Which would include looking for guys that could be potential husbands and thinking, "maybe he's the one" when you meet someone new. (Yes, we all do it – including myself…) When you do meet someone, instead of thinking it "could be him" – which is hard to do if you have done it awhile - simply praise

God He allowed you to meet one of your brothers in the Lord who love and serve Him faithfully. Ladies, if we are looking, than we are not resting.

We could look at resting in the Lord the following way:

Relying on the Lord's strength and His grace, not your own, to accomplish the task set before you – in this case, contentment.

Entrusting your dreams and desires to the Lord, bringing them under His lordship and leaving them at His feet.

Serving selflessly, joyfully and as unto the Lord no matter where you are, no matter what He has you doing.

Trusting Him to bring about His perfect and complete plan for your life in His perfect and complete time.

Remember! God is faithful! Rest is attainable! So go out there and do it!

Contentment is waiting on the Lord with patience. "...Wait patiently for Him..." (Psa. 37:7) Did He have to mention *that* word? Patience is not a strong point, okay. So maybe I'll just mark that part out with dark ink. Ever feel that way? I am the kind of person where everything has to be in place and all my little ducks have to be in a nice neat row and they have to get that way in a very orderly and swift fashion. Ask anyone and they'll be more than happy to verify that statement. However, waiting patiently must be within reach otherwise God would not have said it in His Word.

I guess we can look at it this way. While sitting at a red stoplight, you have to wait for it to turn green so you can continue on down the road. You can do that waiting with two different attitudes. First, you can get frustrated and even sometimes mad that the light isn't turning to green as soon as you'd like (a duck out of line!), or you can wait patiently for it to turn. No matter what your attitude is, every person that has watched a stoplight knows that the light will eventually change. They're programmed and set that way. It will happen. The same is true when we are waiting on God to turn on the go-ahead light from one season of our life to another. We can get frustrated and discouraged for being in the single lane and fight tooth and nail every mile of the road, or we can wait on the Lord with patience for His timing, knowing that He will do what He says He will when the time is right. God says, "I have things under control. I have a plan and purpose for your life. It's been designed since the beginning of the world. The light will turn. I will carry out My plan for you in My time." God said it. Believe it. "I can do all things through Him [Christ] who strengthens me." (Phil. 4:13) Claim it. Patience is possible!

In the journey to arriving at contentment there must be a death. You and I must die to self, our dreams and desires. God gave me three little words when I was really struggling with contentment that for me sum it all up. "Give. It. Up." Give it up to the Lord, lay it at His feet and leave it there. But in order to give it up, I have to die to my heart's desire, and many times this means to die daily. I must take that desire of marriage, die to it, lay it at the Savior's feet and leave it there to fulfill it when He knows is the best time. By dying I mean giving it to God and saying, "This is what I want, but I want instead whatever it is that You have for me, whether that's marriage or singleness." Elisabeth Elliot says, "Human desire is to be brought under the lordship of Christ for fulfillment according to His wisdom and choosing." Before we can get something better, we have to let go of what we have. It's laying down our own desires (self's desires) and picking up God's desire for our lives.

If it weren't possible, God wouldn't ask it of us.

When I take my focus off of Aprill and what Aprill wants, and put that focus on God and what God has for Aprill, it makes the struggle with that "C" thing far less difficult. It's not what I want that counts, but what God has. Believe me, what He has is so much better than what we could ever imagine.

There is a battle. On one side of the battlefield is self's desires. On the other are God's best desires for us. If self surrenders, there will be peace and self will not be a prisoner of war but instead given contentment, because God would become the focus. If self continues to fight, the war will rage on because self is the focus. Putting your focus on God is way better than anything else!

Now, is this "C" thing possible to attain? Can a person really win the war and come out victorious? Is there any hope whatsoever? Absolutely! If it weren't possible, God wouldn't ask it of us. "…For I have learned, in whatsoever state I am, therewith to be content." (Phil. 4:11 KJV) How? You and I can be content through Jesus Christ our Lord and Savior. God's strength and grace is there for the claiming. I heard someone once say that God has already given us His strength; all we have to do now is take it. So go for it, ladies! Be content in God's perfect plan for you.

However, following right on the heels of contentment is the realization and acceptance of God's gifts to us. We have to remember that when anything comes from God, we know without a doubt that it is good, really good, and that it is a gift. Yes, a gift. Because "every good gift and every perfect gift is from above, and comes down from the Father of lights, with whom there is no variation or shadow of turning." (James 1:17) What we do with that gift is another story. What am I talking about? Keep reading and you'll hear it straight from the Old Maid's mouth! ☺

God asks no man
whether he will accept life.
That is not the choice.
You must take it.
The only choice is how.

Henry Ward Beecher

Chapter 5

The Gift Horse

You've heard the expression, "Don't look a gift horse in the mouth." I've heard it for as long as I can remember, but I never knew exactly what it meant until one day at church. Our pastor was out of town and one of the men in the congregation shared a very encouraging word from the Lord. He explained what it meant to look a gift horse in the mouth.

When you look in a horse's mouth, you're looking at his teeth to see what shape they're in. If they're not real worn down, he's got a lot of years left of work in him. If they're chipped and deteriorated, he doesn't have many years left to his life and therefore, you can't get much out of him. So, to look a gift horse in the mouth would be to see just how good of a gift you were getting and that would be an insult to the giver.

So, what does a gift horse have to do with life in the single lane? Well, that bright sunny Sunday in June was a turning point in my life. It finally clicked what it meant when people said singleness is a gift. I finally could view my singleness, my loneliness, and my life as it was, as a gift and accept it. The thought that I might be driving down the single lane for the rest of my life here on this earth no longer scared me to death. If that was what God had for me, I was okay with it. In fact, I was excited about it. I hoped that the "Marriage" exit wouldn't come for many, many miles yet so I could try out my new perspective!

Allow me to stop for just a minute and remind you that nothing had changed in my situation as a single that Sunday. I was still traveling down the single lane. I was still an old maid. No guy suddenly appeared at church with a big flashing sign saying "I'm the One! Exit now!" No one came up to me and told me that there was a guy hanging in the wings ready to whisk me off to the land of marriage. As far as I could tell there was absolutely no possibly that the "one" God had for me was coming anytime soon. So when I say that I accepted the gift of singleness as a gift from the Lord Jesus on that day, I am not saying so because the trial had passed and I then could view things with 20/20 vision. Once you're out of the fire, you can calmly say what wonderful things God did for you and how it all was for the best. But when you're in it, that is the farthest thing from your mind as you are being stretched to your limit. Our reaction should be to give thanks in everything, but in our human nature, we fall short and most of the time do the exact opposite of what God tells us to. The unknown was still lurking before me. I didn't have any revelation of what my life was going to be in the future. I didn't have a clue. There was no billboard on the side of the road with my name on it advertising how many miles until the next "REST" area – Reliable Extensive Singleness Termination. I had no guarantee that if I said, "Yes singleness is a gift, Lord, I accept it as such," then I would marry soon. I simply accepted the gift God had given to me, for as long as God saw fit for me to have it.

Could this really be a gift?

Now wait a minute! Being companionless, a gift? Being lonely, a gift? Being left behind, a gift? Driving down the single lane, a gift? Not being able to love and stand by and cherish and be a helpmate to a Godly man, a gift? Not being cherished by that wonderful guy, a gift? You're thinking, "This lady is crazy! She has totally lost it! Someone revoke her license!" Before you close the book and never look at it again, keep reading, I think you'll change your mind.

First, I have to confess that it always bothered me to no end when people would tell me that my singleness was a gift, when it was a married person telling me that. The thought that normally ran through my head would be, "Easy for you to say, you're married." Usually it was someone who at my age was already married and had at least a couple kids. Marriage was something I wanted so bad that I couldn't see the potential of my singleness.

Before it clicked, just about every time I heard of a friend or acquaintance that was getting married who was younger than I was, I would go from one extreme to the other. First I would ask myself, "Why are they getting married and not me? I am way more qualified and ready than they are – look how old I am and what I've done to prepare!" It's terrible and wrong to do that, but I did it. The other extreme was to say, "What's wrong with me? I mean look how young they are and they have it all together, but I don't! Something is wrong with me!" Both of these perspectives stem from pride, are lies from the devil, and, might I add, totally against God's Word. When I do this I am not only comparing myself to someone else, but I am also questioning God's distribution of gifts to His children.

There it is again – a gift. Uh-huh! Right! Let me explain.

We, as imperfect sinful human beings, don't deserve anything but to be forever separated from God and burning in the lake of fire. Romans chapters three and six say that all have sinned and come short of the glory of God and that the wages of that sin is death – eternal separation from God. The Bible also says that we cannot do good things in order to be good enough to enter into Heaven. Things look pretty hopeless for us until Jesus enters the picture. He took our place and died for our sins, paying the penalty for those sins. We don't deserve the gift of eternal life He so freely gives us because we are the guilty ones. Nevertheless, because of God's love for us, He sent Jesus to die that we might live. We can accept this gift or reject it, that is our choice. We are undeserving of any good thing and definitely not entitled to anything good. Therefore, anything that comes from God is a gift. Including singleness.

We can accept this gift or reject it...

Now, there is a big difference between seeing singleness as a gift and accepting it as such. Just as we can see and understand that God has given the gift of salvation through Jesus Christ, it's not until we accept that gift as our own does it do any good.

As the years went by and I moved further away from my ideal marrying age, I could see how my singleness could be a gift because of all the things I was able to do for God that I wouldn't have been able to do if I was married. But I never had a peace about it until I accepted the gift as my own and stopped looking the gift horse in the mouth and stopped resenting the lane I was driving in. By questioning God's holy judgment in giving me such a gift, by balking and complaining about my situation ("Lord, why aren't I married?"), I was looking the gift horse in the mouth and God was the giver. Ouch!

"...But each one has his own gift from God, one in this manner and another in that." (1 Cor. 7:7) Marriage is a gift, and singleness is a gift. One is not inferior to the other nor is one of greater price and value than the other. Believe me, I am sure there is a rooting section for the singles with that statement because over and over again it's portrayed that marriage is above singleness – it's not blatantly of course, but subtly. You have arrived if you're married. If you're not married nor have a boyfriend, then something must be wrong with you. Not hardly! If you are single, God has just given you a different gift for this season of your life. It may change and He may give you the gift of marriage, but it doesn't lessen the gift of singleness.

One is not inferior to the other.

Allow me to pause for just a moment to caution you to never have the mindset that marriage is above singleness, especially when it does come time for you to marry. There is nothing more irritating to me than a girl (who has found a guy) that is snobbish and snotty to her single friends and acquaintances because she's getting married. You know the ones I'm talking about. To use an old expression, they put on airs. They have the attitude that they've arrived and are better than you. I have an understanding with my best friend and family that if I ever act in such a fashion, they are to hit me beside the head so hard my feet will sting. After I told my best friend I hoped I'd never be like that, she replied without skipping a beat, "You won't 'cause I won't let you." Remember that one gift is not superior to the other.

One time when my pastor was praying for me, he said something that I need to be reminded of and keep a close eye on. He thanked the Lord that I was content in my singleness, etc., but then he asked the Lord to help me not to be cocky about it. He hit the nail on the head firmly and completely. I shouldn't be cocky about being content or about having the gift of singleness. "Pride goeth before destruction, and an haughty spirit before a fall." (Pro. 16:18 KJV) Ouch! Beware! If you are anything like me, it is a good reminder to have.

Okay. Ecclesiastes says there is a time for everything under the sun and that the Lord will make everything beautiful in His time. Today, right here, right now, I am in the single lane and it is not because something is wrong with me or that I am overqualified or underqualified, it is simply not God's time for me to be married. If you are in the single lane, right now, right here, today, than it is not God's time for you to be married either. He has given you and me the gift of singleness and He has a purpose for you and me being in that single state. God knows best. He said it. Believe it. Elizabeth Barrett Browning said, "God's best gifts put man's best dreams to shame." How true it is!

God will still give me the gift of singleness regardless of my reaction to it. I can take it because I have to and stick it in a closet somewhere, wasting my energy wrestling with that "C" thing, or I can accept it with a grateful heart, opening it up, using it to it's fullest potential. When I put it to use, I'm not wasting something God has entrusted to my care. I am being a good steward. Again, it is our attitude toward it. Accept it and there will be peace. Reject it, looking the gift horse in the mouth and there will be war. I've been there, done that and got the bumper sticker! Let's rejoice in what God has blessed us with declaring, "Thou hast dealt well with Thy servant, O LORD, according to Thy word." (Psa. 119:65)

"Thou hast dealt well with Thy servant, O Lord!"

Girls, God wants to do something spectacular, something so awesome and exciting in your life it's beyond your imagination! But you have to let Him do His work to carry out His perfect plan. "Well I am," you say. But if you arc wishing for something else, anything else besides what God is doing in your life right now, than you are not letting Him work. You have to step aside in order for God to step forward. Getting in God's way is a sure way to complicate your life, but getting out of God's way is a sure way to simplify it. So embrace what God is doing right now, right here, today. Embrace His gift, His plan, His purpose for your life and watch as He carries out awesome things in you and through you. And once you have stepped forward in His plan, don't look back, stand back or hold back. Give God your all. Believe me, if God has called you to it, whatever it is, is hands-down awesome, mighty, worth it and oh so good! So go do it! Turn up the radio and drive down that single lane with a joyful heart!

The next thing to deal with would be that not-so-fun-but-again-good-for-you thing called waiting. Oh great! Not that! Anything but that! Please! Yes, I know what you're thinking, because remember you're getting it straight from the Old Maid's mouth! ☺

Faith is not believing that God can, but that God will!

Abraham Lincoln

Chapter 6

The Waiting Scene

"What do you mean you *don't* have a boyfriend? You *don't* date either? What's that? Say again! You're *what*? 'Waiting on God!?'"

One can get several reactions to the statement "I'm waiting on God in regards to my marriage partner." You can sometimes get a reaction that's funny, but most of the time it's a discouraging one when people look at you like you've just stepped off the planet Mars and left your brains behind. Or they might even voice their opinion and tell you it is a crazy idea if not totally and completely insane (they do so of course in a tactful and semi-polite way). "You're not out looking? How are you suppose to meet someone if you're not out where there's guys?" Some might tell you, "You know, dearie, God helps those who help themselves." But no, that philosophy is a huge misconception. God does not need our help. He can handle it and, let's be serious, He has been handling things quite well for a lot of years now. He has proven Himself faithful time and time again. So it is okay, go ahead and "Wait for the LORD; Be strong, and let your heart take courage; Yes, wait for the LORD." (Psa. 27:14)

But what exactly is the meaning of waiting on God? I'm learning that the first step is to take my eyes off of me and put them back on Jesus. When I focus on my life and how I think or want things to be, I have lost sight of Jesus and taken my eyes off of Him and His plan for me. I need to view things through His eyes, not mine. He has better vision and a bigger and broader view. God has big plans for my life and yours, but unless we submit and follow after Him in every area of our lives, we will never reach our fullest potential for Him. When we surrender to Him, great things will happen. His capable hands will produce spiritual treasures in our lives. Trusting Him and relying fully and totally on Him is the ultimate place to be. Nothing gets better than that.

Nothing gets better than this!

I have also learned that waiting is not sitting on the side of the road with my car hood up, twiddling my thumbs, anxiously waiting for some guy to show up out of the blue and into my life. Waiting does require an action. No, I am not talking about going out with a great big stick and beating the bushes, snatching the first guy that pops out – what kind of guy are you going to find hiding in the bushes anyway!? (Besides, using such a method might hurt someone.) I don't mean going out and visiting every church in the country inspecting the flock. (This would take way too long, there are way too many churches. By the time you got through the ones just in your home state, you would have to have plastic surgery to repair the squint lines around your eyes.) And, no, you don't have to go to every single's group in your city. (Though it would not take as long as the previous idea, it's still not what I'm talking about.) No this action is something that my flesh doesn't necessarily want to do (which means it's good for me). I have to consciously, purposefully and willfully put it into motion. Believe me, it's one of those times when the spirit is willing but the flesh is oh so weak – there is a huge "S" roadblock in the way. This action is best described in an acronym for wait.

The **W** stands for **Withstanding** the temptation to put my own desires above God's. When I want my dreams more than I want God's plans, it becomes an idol to me. We are told in Deuteronomy 5:7, "You shall have no other gods before Me." If we want something more than what God wants, then that something is more important to us than God and thus an idol.

We don't need to throw our dreams away, but give them to God instead for safekeeping. In His perfect timing and according to His infinite wisdom, if and when He sees fit, He will make them come true. Our prayer should be that God would make His desires for us our desires. Our desires and dreams need to line up with God's. Remember, His plans are way better than ours, His map infallible.

The **A** stands for **Accepting** the gift God has blessed me with for this season of my life. No questions asked. Don't look the gift horse in the mouth. It is definitely easier said than done but making acceptance your goal is absolutely rewarding. God is sovereign. He is El Roi, The God Who Sees. He knows without a doubt why He bestowed upon you the gift He has and that it is His very best for you. God makes no mistakes. There are no holes in His plans. He has a reason for you being in the single lane.

Our desires and dreams need to line up with God's.

The **I** stands for **Investing** my gift, using it for God's glory and not burying it. This includes all my gifts, talents and abilities that God has blessed me with, not just my gift of singleness. To invest means, "to put to use." God does not give us gifts to put on the shelf to look at and never use. He does not ever give us gifts that we personally cannot exercise. Each gift is unique to us because God is the Creator and knows us better than we know ourselves. He does not make any mistakes – big or small. Sometimes we may think He's making a mistake because what He is doing does not make sense to us, but God makes no blunders. Do not make the error Sarah made by laughing at what God says and promises to do. (Genesis 18.1-15) He did what He promised Sarah and He'll do what He promises us. He said He only does things for our good. Believe it. When He says He is going to give you a particular gift, He is not making a goof-up. Use it as He intended you to. Do not waste it. Be a good steward of what God has given.

The **T** stands for the **Transforming** work God will do in my life when I totally rely on Him for my every need, wants and desire. God gives us what we need not necessarily what we want. If we are not married right now, then a husband is not something we need at this time. It does not mean we will never need one at some point in our lives, it is just not during this season of our lives. Girls, be "confident of this very thing, that He who began a good work in you will perfect it until the day of Christ Jesus." (Phil 1:6) A potter never stops working on the clay until he is confident that the piece is the best. God is the Potter and we are the clay, so He will continue to work in our lives, molding and shaping us to be like Jesus, until we bow before His throne in Heaven.

Be encouraged! Waiting is not done alone. When we usually think of waiting, it is in reference to waiting for someone to show up. But is this the case in waiting on the Lord? Absolutely not! "But they that wait upon the LORD shall renew their strength; they shall mount up with wings as eagles; they shall run, and not be weary; and they shall walk, and not faint." (Isa. 40:31 KJV) I have read this verse over and over again, but the other day I was reading it again and it hit me differently than ever before. When I read "wait upon the LORD," I had this picture of my head resting *upon* God's chest. And I realized waiting on the Lord is not waiting by myself, but *with* Him, *upon* Him. It makes perfect sense! "For He [Jesus] hath said, 'I will never leave thee nor forsake thee.'" (Hebrews 13:5b KJV) If He says He will *never* leave me nor forsake me, why would He break His word and leave me to wait alone? I'm not waiting for Him, but on Him to carry out His plan for my life. So driving in the single lane isn't done single-handedly, but with Jesus! I don't know about you, but that is way neato!

Waiting is not done alone...

However, there is another action that goes hand in hand with waiting. Faith. Do I have the faith to believe that God does know what He's doing and that He has given me all that I need right now? You see "...faith is the substance of things hoped for, the evidence of things not seen." (Hebrews 11:1 KJV) Do what Proverbs 3:5 and 6 says and trust in the

Lord with all your heart, leaning not on your own understanding, but in all your ways, acknowledge Him and He will direct your paths. He is trustworthy – no doubt about it!

Take courage, my friend, and wait upon the Lord. Do not stop on the side of the road, get out your big stick and beat the bushes for whatever and whoever pops out. And don't flip through the phone book to look up the local church listings! Avoid the "S" detour like the plague and you are free to wait with and upon the Lord! It is possible! Hey, you've heard it straight from the Old Maid's mouth! ☺

God's heavenly plan
doesn't always make
earthly sense.

Charles Swindoll

Chapter 7

Sensible Solution to a Senseless Situation

All you've ever wanted to do is get married and be a homemaker, raising your children in the Lord. Other girls are going to college and getting a career. And out of these two categories of girls, which one seems to be producing a married one? Yep, you guessed it. It seems that the girls getting married around you are the ones going for those letters after their names. It doesn't make any sense! Lord, all I want to do is be what you have called women to be…homemakers! And I'm not the one getting married. I am perpetually driving down a never-ending, unceasing, spinsterish lane. What is up with this!?

When I voiced this frustration to a friend of mine, she calmly reminded me that God rains on the just and on the unjust alike. Now, that doesn't mean that girls in one category are just and the other are unjust, but that God sometimes rains on someone else when we think He should rain on us. There is no partiality with God.

Despite our inability to get into God's mind and figure out what it is He's planning, there is something we can do about our senseless situation. We can trust.

"Never be afraid to trust an unknown future to a known God."

Trust is about putting your faith in God about that which you can't see, perceive, understand, grasp or when things just don't make any sense whatsoever and your understanding and rational have failed. "Now faith is the substance [assurance] of things hoped [trusted] for, the evidence [proof] of things not seen." (Heb 11:1, KJV) Faith is about trusting God in the unknown. If we know it already, there is no reason to trust, believe, rest or rely upon the Lord. "…Hope [faith or expectation] that is seen is not hope: for what a man seeth, why doth he yet hope for?"(Rom. 8:24, KJV) Corrie ten Boom encourages us by saying, "Never be afraid to trust an unknown future to a known God." We may not know what is down the road, but God does – He planned it, created it and it is good.

Here is a way to define trust:

The **T** is for **Tasting** and seeing that the Lord is good (Psa. 34:8). "The LORD is good to all…" (Psa. 145:9) No matter what. Because God is good everything He does is good. That is just who God is. He is the same yesterday, today and forever (Hebrews 13:8). In order to trust, you have to have a right view of God and who He is. Believing Him, taking Him at His word. Knowing He won't ever let you down. Believing He will do everything according to His character. God is not going to do something that is a contradiction to His character or His Word. Doubting what He says is not trusting. If you have a distorted view of God, it does not allow you to trust Him completely and unconditionally.

The **R** is for **Relinquishing** your will, desires and dreams to Him. If we hold on to what we want or think we want, there is no room for what God has for us. I guess that means we're back to giving everything up to Him - wholly, utterly, entirely, completely. Give it all or don't give it at all. It is all or none and none for all – your nothingness, His everything. C.S. Lewis said, "To walk out of his [God's] will is to walk into nowhere."

The **U** is for **Understanding** that He has your best in mind and that His plan is the best one for your life. Whatever is going on, whatever kind of traffic jams you find yourself in, rest assured that it will work out for God's glory and your good, because that is a promise that He's made. Remember Romans 8:28? "All things work together for good…" And God doesn't go back on His promises. He keeps every one of them. He said it. Believe it. As C.S. Lewis also said, "God allows us to experience the low points of life in order to teach us lessons we could learn in no other way." 1 Peter 5:10 says, "But the God of all grace, who hath called us unto his eternal glory by Christ Jesus, after that ye have suffered a while, make you perfect, establish, strengthen, settle you." (KJV)

The **S** is for **Standing** firm in who you are in Christ Jesus and in what He has called you to do through His strength. Put on that armor He has given to you and go out and accomplish what He has called you to. It doesn't matter what the circumstances are or the trials that come at you. He who has called you is faithful. Stand firm in that. Stand firm in Him. "Finally, be strong in the Lord, and in the strength of His might. Put on the full armor of God, that you may be able to stand firm against the schemes of the devil. For our struggle is not against flesh and blood, but against the rulers, against the powers, against the world forces of this darkness, against the spiritual forces of wickedness in the heavenly places." (Ephesians 6:10-12)

This **T** is for **Totally** and utterly relying on Him, His strength, His grace, His peace, His joy, and His comfort. Leave everything in His hands. He is capable of handling any situation, any hardship, any confusing thing that will and can happen in your life and in the lives of those around you. Nothing is too big or too small for God to handle.

Another thing we need to remember is what Philippians 4:19 says, "And my God shall supply all your needs according to His riches in glory in Christ Jesus." Yes, God will supply, furnish, satisfy, accomplish, complete, fulfill and perfect your every need. Matthew 6:8 says, "...for your Father knows what you need, before you ask Him." But notice it doesn't say, "God will supply your every want." There is a difference between the two – a BIG one!

God supplies your needs, not your wants...

In one of Elisabeth Elliot's books, she said that if God doesn't give it to you, then you don't need it. Therefore, if I don't have a husband right now, then I don't need one. I may want one, but remember, need and want are two different things. You may feel lonely and feel like you need someone just to give you a hug, but if God doesn't send someone to give you that hug, then you must not need it as much as you think you do.

Now this is where I say, "Ouch!" When I realized I needed to apply this idea in a smaller sense, I would have cried had I been by myself. I greatly struggle with this one because I am one of those people who love to get and give hugs. Physical touch is one of my love languages so I like LOTS of hugs. But if God doesn't send someone to give me those hugs, then they are a want, not a need. And that is so hard for me to swallow when I feel like I "need" someone to give me a good hug. (I want to cry just writing about it.) God promises that He will supply our every need. Therefore you and I have to claim that and believe He will do just exactly as He says. God said it. Believe it. (And I'm unmistakably talking to myself too!)

"God's will ought to be our aim, and I am quite contented that His designs should be accomplished and not mine."

One of my heroes is Robert E. Lee, General of the Confederate Army. He said, "God's will ought to be our aim, and I am quite contented that His designs should be accomplished and not mine." May it be true in my own life and in yours.

Never forget that God is the sensible solution to any senseless situation. He can handle everything that comes His way. He is never surprised, never alarmed, never at a loss for what to do next. He is the Driver who is always prepared for any kind of road conditions. When you feel like things just don't make any sense whatsoever, give it to the Lord and it will be all right. And you've heard it straight from the Old Maid's mouth! ☺

I know that there is nothing better for them than to rejoice, and to do good in one's lifetime.

Ecclesiastes 3:12

Chapter 8

Seasons

Don't you just love the seasons? Spring, Summer, Fall, Winter. Each one brings with it so much diversity. There is a different feel to the air as spring approaches after a long cold winter. As you drive along, you see patches of green grass poking through the earth. Things really begin to warm up as spring turns into summer – and it's either turn on the air conditioner or roll the windows down! With fall, the flowers start to fade away and the leaves of the trees turn bright orange, red and yellow, creating a beautiful scene out every window of your car. There are different advantages and drawbacks to each, yet without them our lives would not be as we know it. Some people like winter, others summer, others spring and still others fall. No matter which one you like the best, seasons come and seasons go.

Life is full of seasons too. There are the seasons of childhood, young adult years (or what some would call teen years), and adult years. Then there are the seasons of kindergarten, elementary, high school, and college. Each of these is predictable in how long they will last and what they will contain.

"Time is so precious that God deals it out only second by second."

The seasons that are not foreseen are the seasons of singleness, married life, and widowhood. Of these only God knows their duration. For some people, one season will last for years, while for other people it will only last days. Bishop Fulton J. Sheen reminds us, "Time is so precious that God deals it out only second by second." Living each day at a time is good advice even when there is not a crisis going on.

Solomon said, "To everything there is a season, A time for every purpose under heaven. A time to be born, and a time to die…a time to weep, and a time to laugh; a time to mourn, and a time to dance…a time to embrace, and a time to refrain from embracing…a time to get, and a time to lose…a time to love, and a time to hate." (Eccl. 3:1, 2a, 4, 5b, 6a, 8a KJV) And in all this, God "hath made everything beautiful in His time." (Eccl. 3:11a KJV)

As we go through each season of our lives, driving down each unique lane, hold to the promise that it is all beautiful. Each season, every moment, each breath we take is a gift from God. Do not take any of them for granted. Don't wish for one season (your singleness) to hurry up and be over with so you can get on with the next one (marriage). Isn't it funny how we think that one season should as a rule go faster than the others? Life in the single lane should be a quick journey, while the lane of marriage should go on forever, and the lane of widowhood should have a "Road Closed" sign across the roadway at all times. But being content in each season and living life to its fullest potential for God is what makes it beautiful. Accept it, embrace it and hold on to it with a passion because God gave it to you. If you are single, don't waste your time wishing to be married. If you're married, don't waste your time wishing you weren't. Doesn't that sound like a terrible thing to say? So why does it sound so strange telling you not to wish away the gift of singleness? Remember! If God gave it to you, it's good and He has you in that season for a reason. There is a time for everything and only God knows when and how to bring you into the next season of your life. He knows best.

In each season, focus on doing whatever it is that God has for you to do during that time. Don't look for tomorrow and what it may bring, tomorrow may never come. "Tomorrow's life is too late. Live today." (Martial) Just like I said before, life doesn't start when you get married. Life started the day you were conceived. If you are waiting to live life after the next season starts, you are dead already - the opposite of living is death. The "C" thing plays such a major role in our lives. Everything ties together doesn't it?

Okay, let's get practical. Let's say that you really, really want to get married and you are struggling with that "C" thing. However, you are still in school. God has given you a job – school – for this season of your life. Focus on accomplishing the task set before you and when you have completed it God will bring the next thing He has for you. Now, that may or may not include a husband, but know that it will be the very best.

"Tomorrow's life is too late. Live today."

Let's say you are graduated but still at home with your parents and siblings. There is always tons of things to do (you just don't have a fancy name to sum up all that you do during the day). Whatever you have to do today is the job you need to focus on. Catching up on laundry, baking the bread, helping your younger siblings with their school or chores, cleaning, writing, etc. (I can't even list all that one does there's so much that keeps you busy!) Again, this is a season! Do it as unto the Lord!

No matter what you are doing, no matter where God has you right now, it is important to Him. Focus on accomplishing the task for today and there will be no time to worry about or wish for tomorrow. "Therefore do not worry about tomorrow, for tomorrow will worry about itself. Each day has enough trouble of its own." (Matt. 6:34 NIV®) A. J. Cronin said, "Worry never robs tomorrow of its sorrow, but only saps today of its strength."

So as Jonathan Swift said, "May you live all the days of your life." Be encouraged in what God has for you and take it straight from the Old Maid's mouth! ☺

10

The king's daughter is all glorious within: her clothing is of wrought gold.

Psalm 45:13 KJV

Chapter 9

My Precious Daughter

One night I was feeling especially discouraged over my singleness. The desire to marry was so great and I felt like no one really understood where I was coming from, except perhaps my best friend who is in the same boat as me. It was about eleven o'clock at night and things couldn't have looked worse. But the Lord reminded me that He understood better than anyone else ever could, even more than I did. I felt compelled to write the following letter. God gave me a big hug and reassured me that all would be well because He is faithful. I share it with you in hopes that you too will see how much our Abba Father loves and cares for us, the King's daughters.

My Dearest Daughter,

I know what you are feeling tonight. I can feel the anguish, the sadness and, yes, even the longings of your heart. I know how much you desire to marry, to become a wife and mother. I know your struggles to be still and rest in Me. I know it's hard. I see your tears - those that fall when no one else sees. I feel your pain. I hear your cries. I'm listening. I understand. I'm here. I love you with an everlasting love that cannot be compared to the love of any other. And because of this love, My thoughts and plans for you are so awesome, so special and beautiful, you cannot imagine them in all your wildest imaginations. I am so excited when I think about all I have in store for you. I can hardly contain myself! Oh what I have designed for you! It is nothing like anything I have ever planned for anyone else – it is so unique and specially designed for you and only you. It is going to be awesome, so wonderful you'll stand back in awe and amazement at its beauty. My precious, precious daughter, there is one thing I must ask of you first, but it is the only requirement I have. You must trust Me - ardently and completely - to carry out all I have planned. And in order for you to trust Me, you must leave everything totally to Me. You cannot try to make something happen or even "help" Me along. Don't worry. I've been doing this for a very long time. I can handle it. So wait. Wait and rest in Me. Be content. I only have the very best in mind for you. I will not withhold any good thing from you. My timing is perfect. Now I know it might not be what you would consider "ideal" but I see it all - the big picture - and I know the perfect time to make it really, really spectacular. I know you've dreamed of what seems to be the perfect, most spectacular story, but I know you so much better than you know yourself and I know what's best for you. I am your Creator. I have formed you and made you who you are. And you are so beautiful in My eyes. You are My little girl. I love you. Yes, even before I knit your tiny frame together in your mother's womb, I loved you. There is nothing that can separate you from My love. I am all you need. I am the One who fills you with overflowing joy. I will never, never let you down. I know you sometimes feel alone, but I am always here, holding you in My arms. I never leave. I am faithful - you can count on Me. So don't get discouraged. Give Me your fears, your anxieties, your deepest desires. Trust Me. I will do great and mighty things in your life if you let Me.

All My Love,

Abba Father

I am old, advanced in age.

Joshua 23:2

10 Chapter

The Old Maid Complex

It was a bright warm day, the sun's rays beating down upon the small town in the southwestern desert. It wasn't too hot yet, but promised to be by the afternoon.

I was busy pushing the toddler swing, the little boy in the seat swaying back and forth with the most precious grin on his little face. I'd push him high and he'd say, "'Gin!" The swing would go flying and his giggle could be heard around the yard. "'Gin!" and off into the air he'd go. One of his sisters was swimming in the small pool in the middle of the grass. Splashes of water jumped out of the pool. His other sister was sitting on a chair nearby.

The five-year-old girl had an inquisitive look on her face. After a few minutes, she voiced what she was thinking. "Are you married?" she asked me curiously.

"No," was my reply.

"Have you ever been married?"

"No."

A moment or two passed as I pushed the little boy in the swing.

Her look was somewhat disbelief. "How *old* are you?"

"Twenty-two."

Surprise registered on her face, then what you might call understanding. "Oh," she said matter of fact, "you're too old to get married - you have to be seventeen to get married."

"Seventeen?" I echoed with amusement.

Her red head bobbed. "Or fifty."

I had to laugh. What is it they say? "Out of the mouth of babes." I hoped it wasn't true. However, it became a joke in my family that since I missed the first number I would just have to try for the second. Hmmm, I'm not even half way there yet - if I let myself, I could get depressed.

Wait a minute! The age between seventeen and fifty…is that when you're an old maid? I didn't think to ask my little friend.

Ever feel like you're getting older and older and more like an old maid? Okay, so you're really not that old – it's all about perspective, right? Three years past twenty, not seven years until thirty. I think at some point in time, no matter what age you are you feel like you're getting older and time is running out. Probably sounds pretty crazy to some people, but if you've been there you know exactly what I mean. I can remember feeling that way when I was eighteen. (Yeah, five years ago – think about how I feel now!? Just kidding!)

I was talking and praying with one young woman about being single, content, wanting to marry and such and the Lord had to remind me to be compassionate and understanding. Why? Because when she told me how old she was and a little of her situation, I was shocked. How could she be so upset and distraught when she hadn't even finished high school yet? She hadn't even experienced what it was like to be out of school and wondering what you were going to do for the rest of your life. She hadn't even reached twenty yet, much less my age! Thankfully the Lord's grace is sufficient and just in time He gently reminded me of when I was her age and felt the exact same way she was feeling. I was then able to relate to her and minister to her the way she needed.

You see, no matter how old or, depending on who you ask, how young you are, it is very possible to feel like an old maid. Oh, you know you're not old, but sometimes it just feels that way. And whether or not you remember those days in your life, we need to be sensitive to the way other girls may be feeling, encouraging them in any way we can. God is faithful. God is sufficient. He will get each and every one of us through those hard days. We may have realized that singleness is a gift, and also accepted it as such and are winning the battle against the "S" thing, and we're happily driving down the single lane, but there are times when you are blue instead of the sky. Be of good courage! You are not alone and God understands your feelings and is there to help you through the rough times. You are not too old, too young or too in-between. You are exactly the age God wants you to be. You are just right. Besides, "Birthdays are good for you. Statistics show that the people who have the most live the longest." (Reverend Larry Lorenzoni)

"Birthdays are good for you. Statistics show that the people who have the most live the longest."

I have to say though, that in our day, I don't think we have to worry about any certain age when we'll be considered an old maid in the eyes of society. Some might think we've been traveling down the single lane far too long and it's high time for us to be getting married, but I don't think anyone will come right out and call us "old maids" and seriously mean it! (...But then again they might...) My Grandpa gave me and my cousin exactly one-year to find some guys or he would find them for us. When that year came and went, he was gracious enough to give us an extension. He didn't give us a deadline this time so hopefully we will be safe until God sends the right ones along. So even though there have been times some have hinted at us being old maids, very few have out and out called us such! (Brothers, however, are definitely part of that "few"!) But hopefully you won't get that title (unless of course you give it to yourself!), for you really aren't that old, no matter how old or young you are! Yes, you guessed it! You've heard it straight from this old maid's mouth! ☺

Make your life a mission...

not an intermission.

Arnold Glasgow

Chapter 11

Sending Out An SOS

Help! Help! Help! Someone send out an SOS! Oh wait! Look out, I see one! Stand aside, here she comes, driving down the single lane fast and furious with a purpose firmly in place. The Creator of the Universe has carefully mapped out her destination. She lacks nothing for her journey for His sufficiency is more than she will ever need along the way. What is she? An SOS – Single of Service.

Allow me to reiterate the caution not to wait for life to start at marriage. I used to have the mindset that real life did not start until you were married and had a husband and children to care for. All the exciting stuff happened when you were among those in the Sea of Un-Single. Well, I was wrong. Really,

really wrong. Life starts the day you are conceived. “For Thou didst form my inward parts; Thou didst weave me in my mother's womb.” (Psa. 139:13) Life is right now. It’s not tomorrow, next week, next year or even when you reach a certain age. And certainly not when your marital status goes from unmarried to married. If you have been waiting for life to start when you say “I do,” you have lived through part of your life already but didn’t know it. Life is now. So start living! Jump in your car, buckle up, and get ready for the ride of your life!

“…[She] who is unmarried careth for the things that belong to the Lord; how [she] may please the Lord.” (1 Cor. 7:32 KJV) You are single for a reason and that reason is to please the Lord in all that you do and say. How is this done? What a loaded question!

Pleasing God is doing the things that bring Him joy, honor and glory; being obedient to His Word; serving Him. One way to do this is to serve others in the name of our Lord Jesus Christ. “And whatsoever ye do, do it heartily, as to the Lord, and not unto men.” (Col. 3:23 KJV) In the Gospels, Jesus tells us that if we give a cup of cold water to someone in His name, we have given it to him.

What do you say when people ask those famous questions, “What are you doing with your life? Are you going to college or taking some classes or *something*?” My answers to those questions vary depending on the day, week, month and year in which they ask them. One week I'm home doing everyday stuff, but with one phone call, the next week I can be across the state doing something totally different. (And because I'm an SOS – Single of Service – I have that flexibility.) It is so awesome to see what God does when I ask, "Okay, Lord, what would you have me to do next, when would you have me to do it and where would you have me do it?" He is always so faithful to bring the next thing.

Since graduating the end of May in 1999, the Lord has allowed me many opportunities of service and with each one, He does a work in my own life and not just those I serve.

The year following graduation, I had the opportunity to fill in as a receptionist at my dad's office while the permanent receptionist was away. It was a great learning experience. I learned more of how to deal with and interact with other people (adults in the working world). Now, don't get me wrong, I was not suffering from a lack of being socialized because I was home schooled, I simply was able to fine-tune my people skills. My parents and I also thought it was good preparation for me if my future husband ever had his own business. Something else I learned was how much you could brighten someone else's day just by letting the light of Jesus shine through you in your smile, joyful voice and "Have a great day!" at the end of your conversation.

In the Fall of 2000, the Lord blessed me with the opportunity to be a teamleader at an eight week course for young ladies in Dallas called EXCEL – Excellence in Character Education and Leadership. I attended EXCEL as a student right before graduation and was richly blessed by all the wonderful teachings and other activities. (As well as blessed by the friendships of my teammates which continue years later to this day!) But as a leader of eight girls ages 16-18, God did so much more in my life. It was a stretching and growing time. There were so many opportunities for me to have to totally rely on God's wisdom and strength and not try to get by on my own non-wisdom and weaknesses. I learned so much as I served the girls in my care, pointing them to draw near to their Heavenly Father, trusting Him and depending on Him for their every need. I was blessed as I encouraged them to build on the foundation of Jesus Christ, allowing Him to mold and shape them into virtuous women who love God with all their heart, mind, soul, and strength. It definitely was a time when I was blessed by being a blessing.

A month after getting home from EXCEL, I moved three and one half-hours away from home to live with my grandma. Grandpa had died three years previously so she was all alone and I became a companion to her. Our relationship grew and deepened like it had never been before. I got to know her so much better and I would not trade that for anything. I was also able to be a light and witness to her and the entire family – it was said that there was a concern that I would win her to Jesus without saying a word!

Also during that year, the Lord opened the door for me to serve during the day at the local pregnancy crisis center. I went there wanting to help out in any way and ended up being the Assistant Director's assistant. It was so neat to see how God had used everything else that I had learned up until that point in my life, to prepare me for the job that I did. It was an awesome year. I not only greatly enjoyed the time there, but I was privileged to work with and learn from some wonderful women of God. Isn't God good!?

Other things that I did during that year was bless a home school family in making two special graduation presents for their graduating son and daughter. They were remembrance quilts where I placed sentiments that their friends and family had written right onto a quilt I made. A friend did this for me for my graduation and it's something I treasure to this day. That year, I was also able to help give a toddler shower for the Assistant Director of the center. I put into practice things I had learned from EXCEL and it turned out great. I love giving showers and anniversary parties and such – hospitality is definitely right up my alley.

I moved back home the first of 2002. My parents needed me, and because serving starts at home, I went. Allow me to say that one does not need to go about the country or even next door to serve others if you cannot first serve at home. Serving at home *is* a ministry - a very honorable and noble one. Don't ever let somebody tell you any differently. If we are not servants at home, we are not servants at all. And if serving at home is where God has called you for this season of your life, praise God! He is proud when we serve Him where He has called us to serve.

I was at home until June. I then had the opportunity to serve and be a blessing by baby-sitting five kids for a week – ages 2-9, I think. Their parents were having a seminar/class-training in Arizona. We had never met before, I only knew the mother's sister, but what could have been awkward the Lord greatly blessed. The kids liked me and I enjoyed them as well.

Serving at home is a ministry – a very honorable and noble one.

Also in June, I was asked to stay with an elderly couple in Alamogordo, NM. They have known our family since my mom was a little girl riding on Mr. Taylor's school bus. At this time, Mrs. Taylor had Parkinson's and was not able to do the things she used to. I was asked to come and do the cooking, cleaning, laundry, shopping, bill paying, drive them to town and to the doctor's, et cetera. During the course of three months, Mrs. Taylor got progressively worse. She went from being able to shower, get dressed and even get up out of a chair on her own to me helping her. The last three weeks of her life, their granddaughter and I gave her twenty-four hour care. The last two weeks, we were blessed with the help of hospice – they are wonderful people! We are thankful that she was able to stay at home until she passed away on September 9th. But I know that the whole reason I was there was not to cook and clean or even feed her or do any of the other things I did, but to lead her to Jesus. We were sitting on the couch one day, talking about death and I said something about being ready to meet the Lord and she said, "Well, I hope I am." I told her, "Ya know you can be sure of that." And then she asked me how and God graciously gave me the words. She prayed the sweetest prayer, right from her heart. Afterwards she said, "He's my Savior and I want everyone to know it!" God is awesome!

After my time there, I took the time to write down the things that I learned by being a blessing. Sometimes as you are going through something, you don't always realize the good things that come out of it. The following is what I wrote:

- By taking care of Mrs. Taylor, I was serving the Lord in a physical/practical/hands-on way – if I do it unto the least of these, I have done it unto Him.
- I learned to react the way I should to things and not the way I feel. To treat others the way I want to be treated.

And this is a good thing to keep in mind not just all the time but especially in relating to the older people in our lives. One day, we too will be older and someone might need to care for us.

- I learned that doing things with a joyful spirit makes the tasks more enjoyable and others are richly blessed by it.
- Serving others means denying my "life" and myself.

Even though I probably already knew these things, it was a good reminder to me of what serving is all about. Putting Jesus first, others second and little ol' me at the very last.

Sometimes, after something is over, you might wonder what God has next for you. I felt the same way. Recorded in my journal seven days after Mrs. Taylor went home to be with the Lord, I wrote this, "Father, thank you for sustaining me and helping me through this time. Now, as everything begins to settle down, please show me what's next. You are faithful and I know you have a perfect plan for my life. Show me what You want me to do. Day by day, help me to trust You and not worry about tomorrow. Fill me back up and revive me. I desire to do Your will, O God. Show me what that is. Make it clear; may there be no doubts. Thank You, Lord! You know my heart's desire. Lord, I want to please and glorify You! I love you, Abba Father! 'Come and see the works of God: he is terrible in his doing toward the children of men.' (Psalm 66:5 KJV)."

He did bring something. Not long after I was busy hosting a reunion with my teammates from EXCEL, then I was house-sitting and was a part of the planning and putting on of my grandparent's fiftieth wedding anniversary, which turned out to be a huge blessing to Grandma and Grandpa.

The first part of the year 2003, I got a call about my great aunt needing someone to stay with her during the daytime until her kids could get home care set up. I started the end of March and my last day was in April. I was a wonderful opportunity and I am blessed to know that I was a light and witness for her family and a blessing to her.

In May, I helped baby-sit four children while their parents took a much needed vacation. I helped with their schooling and ran them to their gymnastics. It was a blessing to them, as well as to me.

The following months continued to bring more opportunities of service – at home and elsewhere.

To sum up my life since graduation would be to say that serving God while driving down the single lane is an awesome reality and a total blessing! None of the things I have just told you about could have been done if my little plan for my life (graduating and immediately thereafter getting married!) had worked out. God's plan is always the best plan. And it always brings about a blessing!

Now, I may sound like a broken record, "It was a blessing," but it is so true! In each of these opportunities, God has turned things around and blessed me, taught me and drawn me closer to Him. Even now, as I do the things He has called me to right now, I can say with open honesty, it is a blessing. God knows what He is doing and He knows the plans He has for me and how I can best serve Him at this moment in time. What Paul told Timothy is instruction for us as well. He said, "Instruct them to do good, to be rich in good works, to be generous and ready to share." (I Tim. 6:18) So get to it! Be that SOS with a purpose! "Life is a coin. You can spend it any way you wish, but you can only spend it once." (Lillian Dickson) Let us say along with Helen Keller, "I will not just live my life. I will not just spend my life. I will invest my life." There really are so many ways a single woman can serve as she flies down the single lane. And remember, "There is no such thing as insignificant service for Christ!" (*Our Daily Bread*, Vol. 48 No. 11, February 29) Yes, you've heard it straight from the Old Maid's mouth! ☺

I, the LORD, have called
You in righteousness,
And will hold Your hand;
I will keep You…

Isaiah 42:6

Chapter 12

Being Confident

The setting is a group of six or seven. A look around the room would reveal a man and his wife, a dating couple, a woman in her thirties with her male friend and an unattached single in her early twenties. They're a group of friends enjoying an evening together. The conversation is light, nothing too serious. What college classes is this one taking, what's the major for that one? Everyone seems at ease and confident in what they're doing with their lives. Except one. She doesn't go to college; never felt called to, but definitely doesn't lack the know-how or ability to further her education beyond high school. Her goal in life other than serving the Lord is to be a homemaker (no college prep required).

As she sits on the soft couch, sipping her ice tea, the beads of sweat from her glass drip onto her lap. A closer look in her eyes shows some discomfort. She prays silently, desperately asking that no one ask her what courses she's taking or even what she's doing these days. The truth is she isn't studying for a bachelor's degree or a master's and she doesn't feel like she has a "real" job since she works for her self-employed dad. Not only that, she lives at home with her parents and doesn't even pay rent, which could be viewed as mooching off of them. No, it's better that no one takes any interest in her life and she just remain quietly in the background, sipping her weak tea. It's not that she's embarrassed by what she does...or doesn't do. She knows she's doing exactly what God wants her to do and she's okay with that. It's not that she's ashamed of her life, because she's not. It's just that she doesn't have a fancy name to call what she does. Her current occupation doesn't sound impressive. What could she say? I'm a bum? She's serving the Lord by serving her family, but in light of society's definition of success, that is just plain weird. Yes everyone in the room is a Christian, but these days the world's ideas are seeping into the church. If you're not going to college, taking classes or holding down a job of some sort, you're not successful. She takes another drink of her tea and hopes no one tries to be nice and include her in the conversation.

This scenario is semi-factual. My best friend related this experience to me during a late night discussion over the phone. I could totally relate with what she was feeling. In such a situation, why is it that we feel inferior to others or we feel bad because we don't take any kind of classes or have a "real" job (whatever that is)? Listening to everyone talk about their classes and degrees and such, my friend said she felt like she should go out and take at least a couple classes on something, *anything*, just so she would have something to contribute if someone wondered what she was studying. It's not that we're ashamed of what we do, because we're not. God has called us to do what we're doing and that's a good thing. So why do we feel the way we do?

Confidence. We concluded that we're not as confident in what God has called us to as we should be. It's learning to please God first and not other people. It's believing without a doubt that whatever it is that God has called us to do, is exactly what we should be doing. Period. To do anything else would be to disobey the Lord and not follow His perfect plan for our lives. But that is so much easier said than done.

Sometimes I feel like it would be better if I had a fancy name for what I do. I have a job so to speak or at least an occupation that keeps me busy, it's just not a conventional one.

I do a lot of different things here and there. When someone needs me to clean their house, watch their children, direct a drama club, house-sit or care for the elderly, they call me. If someone asks me what I do when I'm doing one of those jobs, I don't have a problem answering them. If they happen to catch me when I'm in-between serving opportunities, I feel like a bum – like I don't have an impressive answer to give them. Even if I say that I'm doing some writing, I don't feel like that is an adequate answer – it doesn't seem like a "real" job. Strange I know, but the ideas and misconceptions of society have seeped into my thinking.

Ideas and misconceptions of society have seeped into my thinking.

Just today I had a lady ask me where it was that I work. I replied (rather lamely) that "I don't, well that is to say that I do some certified payroll work from home, but with the new year I won't be doing it anymore. Oh and I also do some writing." Okay, that sounds really intelligent and I said it so eloquently. Right. I felt like such a nitwit. My mom is the one who pointed out that I was writing this very book to minister to young women and encourage them to do what God has called them to do and even have done a workshop for home school girls. Why couldn't I say what I am doing with the confidence that what I am doing is exactly what God wants me to be doing right now?

Why did I feel like a failure, a bum or some lazy good for nothing? Because she said, "Where are you *working*?" For some odd reason that word (along with the word "college") flusters me. What goes through my mind in the millisecond that goes by from the time they finish asking the question to the opening of my mouth, is the idea that they expect me to be working (or going to college), therefore what are they going to think of me when they find out I don't? Well at least I don't feel like I'm working – not working how most people think of working. Why would such a thing go through my mind? A serious lack of confidence and a fear of man – the desire to please man.

I suppose that the outlook on life and success that most people have (and sadly enough this includes the church) is that your life doesn't amount to much if you don't have an education –which is another word for college degree – or you don't have a career. If your life doesn't fall into one of these categories, you're nothing or at least you are not doing anything productive with your life. It's sad, but unfortunately that is the reaction of many people.

We (and this definitely includes me since I don't seem to comprehend this one quite yet) need to be able to say what we are doing, whatever it may be, with as much pride and confidence as a woman who has climbed the corporate ladder to CEO does. Why? Because God has called us to it.

Isn't it interesting to see the look on a person's face when they ask you what you do and your answer is something other than going to college, taking classes or working somewhere? For a few heart beats they just might be speechless before they go, "Oh…th-that's nice. Are you going to at least take some classes or *something*?"

What if a girl's answer is, "I live at home with my family and serve them"? The other person should never follow that statement up with the common one-liner, "You don't go to college or take some classes or have a job or *something*?" This girl, bless her, is doing exactly what God has called her to for that season in her life. And that should be good enough. Her answer should never be followed up with "You don't have a job outside the home?"

Whatever it is that God has called you to, is a job.

And not only that, but also you and I need to view what we do as a job – whatever we're doing whenever we're asked these questions. "I'm a writer, currently working on a nonfiction book geared towards young women, encouraging them to follow God's plan for their life, not their own plan and certainly not someone else's." I need to forget what I think they think I need to be doing and say what God wants me to be doing and has me doing. (Oh! if I could only implant that in my little brain and put it into practice!)

We, as people in general, fail miserably when we give the impression that what someone else is doing is not good enough because it's not the norm or impressive in the eyes of other people. If God has called you to it, that should be a sufficient answer. Today, after my mom expanded on my incompetent answer, the woman was excited about what I was doing. And of course now I feel like more of a nitwit than before and wish I could rewind time to give a confident answer instead of a weak, blundering one. I need to say with confidence and conviction that what I am doing is what God wants me to and not worry about what other people think. I am not here on this earth to do what other people think is right and I am not here to please other people. I am here to do what God has called me to and to please Him.

Unfortunately, I myself have fallen into the trap of asking the famous questions, "Are you going to go to college?" and "Are you working somewhere?" My thinking was that everyone else asked it and the majority of people do go to college or work, so I might as well ask it. However, the Lord has shown me that that line of thinking is inaccurate. The question should be, "So, where does God have you serving?" No matter their answer, my reaction should be one of encouragement for them to continue pressing on in their service to Him. And isn't that really the heart of it? We are called to serve and whatever it is that God calls us to do, we should be serving Him while we do it. "And whatsoever ye do, do it heartily, as to the Lord and not unto men … for ye serve the Lord Christ." (Col. 3:23, 24 KJV)

And that brings us back to being confident. Being confident in the Lord is being confident in doing what He's called you to do. But not only that, part of being confident is also remembering not to feel sorry for myself when I'm the only one in the room who is doing something different than everyone else is.

During a week of vacation Bible school at our church, I was sitting in the craft room one day, cutting out memory wheels. On one side of me there were two married women talking about pregnancy. One was pregnant at the time and she was relating a story of what happened to her one day in the store. On the other side of me were a mom, her newly married daughter and another married woman. They were discussing the newlywed's early stages of pregnancy. Needless to say, I felt left out, left behind, and left in the dust (getting the picture?). The whole evening I seemed to feel bad. As I contemplated it the next morning during my devotional time, I realized why I had been feeling the way I did. I was having a party with myself – and a very pitiful one at that. I felt completely left out because I could not relate or add anything to the conversation. At the time I would have rather gone somewhere else or not been there at all. (What a terrible reaction!)

None of these women even knew how I felt, much less intentionally discussed something I could not relate to. They were sharing their lives. How could I fault them for that? What did I want them to do, not talk about anything I couldn't relate to? How selfish is that! I had to examine my own attitude. I wanted to be able to relate, but I felt left out because I felt sorry for myself because I couldn't relate. But that was not, and is not, any excuse for throwing a dingy pity party for myself. The truth was I felt left out because I was focused on that "S" thing. (Oh yeah, that "S" thing was roaring loudly with indignation that it was abused and mistreated. "Take the 'S' detour, you'll feel so much worse than you already do!") The fact was, I was totally forgetting the gift God, the Creator of the Universe, had given to me and entrusted to me to use for His glory and honor. I was rejecting that gift and balking at what it was that He had called me to. I was not being content or resting in Him and His perfect plan for my life. And I was definitely not confident in Him or what He has called me to. Ouch! Is it just me or does it seem like everything we do or don't do effects everything else in our lives?

Did you ever notice the first two words in the verse that says that God will complete the work He's started in your life?

Philippians 1:6 starts out with two powerful words "Being confident." Of what? "Of this very thing, that he which hath begun a good work in you will perform it until the day of Jesus Christ." (KJV) What an awesome promise!

And we can be confident without being proud by remembering Who it is that is doing the work in our lives, Who has called us to what He has called us and that without Him we *would* be nothing.

Have I said it enough or do I need to say it again? (I honestly don't think any of us could hear it too much, could we? So…) Have confidence of who you are in Christ and what He has called you to do for each season of your life. Whatever it is has been designed and created just for you by the Almighty God and it is good – no, it's down right awesome! So go out there, hold your head up high, speak and act with confidence because you are a daughter of the King of Kings and His work in your life is powerful and what other people think is not relevant! Drive down that single lane like you're driving the coolest convertible ever made! And you've heard it straight from the Old Maid's mouth! ☺

When I was a child,
I used to speak as a child,
think as a child, reason as a child,
when I became a man,
I did away with childish things.

1 Corinthians 13:11

Chapter 13

Single vs. ... Adult?

I was at a party one time with a group of people from church. After the prayer was said, it was announced that the moms and their children should go through the line first. All the moms with little ones moved towards the food while the rest of us hung back. One woman turned to me and said, "Aprill, you and your mom go, you're a child." Needless to say, it ruffled my feathers somewhat because it seems to happen quite a lot. No one thinks you're an adult no matter how old you are unless you're married. It's crazy but true. If there had been a young woman standing right beside me who was married and even younger than me, it would never have crossed anyone's mind to suggest that to her and her mother. The difference between her and myself – the wedding ring on her left ring finger and what it signifies. You might think, "No way!" But unfortunately, it's an all too common occurrence.

At twenty-two (the age at which this happened), I was an adult by everyone's standards. At eighteen you're an adult to the government and you can vote. At twenty-one, you can legally drink alcohol (which I wouldn't and didn't when I turned twenty-one) and run for the office of Representative for your state legislature. The next age where something happens is twenty-five when your vehicle insurance rates go down and you can run for the office of Senator. Then after that I guess it's thirty-five when you can run for President. Then sixty-two when you become a senior citizen and can draw social security.

My point? When is it that one becomes an adult? According to many different people, the answer is when you say, "I do." They may not say that out loud or even coherently think it, but their actions and words suggest it. Look around and you'll find that no matter how young a girl is when she marries (she may be 17 or 70), she's considered an adult and is treated as one – and whether she's mature or not doesn't make a difference. Why is that? What makes people think that way? I guess you'd have to ask them because I honestly don't know the answer. I do know that a person's marital status should not define whether or not they are an adult.

Of course, not everyone thinks that way. I know that the person who said this to me at that gathering knows I'm an adult and treats me as such, but why the comment? I am an adult but yet I'm not? If you have felt a little of the same frustration as I have, I think we need to see things from their perspective. Perhaps for some people it may be hard to treat a woman as an adult when they've known her for practically all her life. It's difficult maybe to realize she grew up. I have found that if you just wait a little while, they will realize you are not a little girl anymore and their treatment of you will change. So hang in there and leave plenty of room for grace!

Another standard for being an adult seems to be when you move out from your parent's home and get a place of your own. I grant you, you have to be responsible and so forth in order to do that just like you do when you get married, but just because you still live at home doesn't mean you're not those things. I am twenty-three and still live at home with my parents; however, a look at my date book will tell you that I only spend about half the year there. (You should see how excited I get when I actually get to sleep in my own bed!!!) Let me say that it is not wrong or a bad thing to be over eighteen and still live at home. It's okay. There's nothing wrong with you, you are not weird and there is no need to feel bad about it.

Our society has portrayed it to be a stigma, but all I can say is, "Society just better get over it," because God doesn't say anything against it. And if God be for us, who can be against us? We are starting something new. It is time to change the way society thinks! Singles living at home: Are you with me!?

I want to lovingly caution us against making any sort of judgment for adulthood based on one's marital status or location of living. Let's get rid of our preconceived ideas that have proven incorrect. Every person is individual and unique as is their situations and what God has for them. So be encouraging!

> *Singles living at home: Are you with me!?*

Girls, it probably could go without saying, but I will say it anyway. Another thing we need to remember is that in order to be treated as an adult, we must first act like one. "Even a child is known by his doings." (Pro. 20:11a, KJV) Therefore, put away childish things as Paul said, "When I was a child, I used to speak as a child, think as a child, reason as a child; when I became a man, I did away with childish things." (1 Cor. 13:11) If you are not acting mature, it's a given no one will treat you as if you are. You have probably heard that you have to earn respect, well the same goes for being treated as an adult. You have to earn it. If you act like a child, you will be treated as one. If you act like an adult, you earn the privilege of being treated as one.

In our house growing up, we never were teenagers. There was no such thing – it simply did not exist. When we came into the "teen" years, we became young adults. The purpose of growing up is to grow up. (What a novel idea!) We were in training to be adults. So, as we were not yet adults, we were young ones instead. It gives a whole different perspective on life if the goal is to become a responsible adult instead of a "teenager." Honestly, I don't even know the meaning of that. I do know that it has so many bad connotations that I personally didn't want to be associated with it when I was between the ages of thirTEEN and nineTEEN. I guess my parent's theory was that they were raising their children to be adults and they expected us to act like it. Being a teenager was never used as any kind of excuse.

So, whether you're seventeen, seventy or seven hundred, if you want to be treated as an adult, act like it so no one has any doubt in their mind on how to treat you. A few will forget and demote you, but try to let it roll off you like water off a duck's back. It can be hard and sometimes frustrating, but it is possible. And don't forget that one's "lane" status (be it the single lane or the married lane) is not the measuring line for being an adult. Hey, you've heard it straight from the Old Maid's mouth! ☺

For as the body is one
and hath many members,
and all the members of that one body,
being many, are one body,
so also is Christ.

1 Corinthians 12:12 KJV

14 Chapter

Singles In the Church

Have you ever tasted a German Chocolate Cake without the frosting? It's no longer a German Chocolate cake! The frosting is what makes the cake, right!? Or how about trying to make yeast bread without the yeast? It doesn't work well, does it? Unless, of course, you're trying to make a blob of cooked dough! (Believe me, I did just that. The dough was just the right consistency and made beautiful loaves, but it didn't rise in the least bit. I wouldn't recommend trying it!) Okay, have you ever ordered a slice of mouth-watering apple pie at a restaurant but requested that they "please hold the apples"? Well, what about taking the singles out of the church? Pretty absurd, but sometimes that's just what happens in the Body of Christ.

Singles in the church get overlooked because they are…well because they are single. A lot of the time I think everyone else doesn't quite know what to do with these unattached people, whereas some churches have gotten a grasp of the concept that it is okay to be in the single lane and have made a place for them.

Now, I am not saying that every church in the world should have a singles group or something of the like. While I am not bashing them, I am also not promoting them – I plead the fifth! I am not equipped to advise you. Let the Holy Spirit be your guide, He is far more equipped in directing you to what He would have YOU to do. I only have an opinion that can be taken or left according to God's direction in your life.

…Well… because they're single…

I personally do not attend singles groups as the norm. When I need encouragement from someone who knows exactly how I'm feeling, I call my best friend. I also have many other single women friends that I can talk to and cry with. I have attended two singles groups that I can remember in my adult life. Each one was interesting in its own way, but I probably wouldn't go back to either one of them. They were just not what I needed at the time. But that's not to say I would never go to anything with the name "singles" on it, because that isn't true. Everyone is different and with that comes different needs. If God has led you to attend a singles get-together or class, then go! If He hasn't, then don't go!

I know it's probably way over stressed that singles groups should not be the place you go to scope out the flock for potential mates, but it is nevertheless an important warning. The focus of any single should be first and foremost to serve the Lord. While some groups are sincere in serving the Lord, others can be the one department Wal-Mart left out of their stores – "Associate assistance requested in the Mate Selection Department, aisle four, please!" Remember why we're driving down the single lane! It's in God's plan for our lives at this moment in time. To try and change our status or exit off the Single Turnpike when God is not turning on the green light, we are stepping out of His will and into trouble.

Also, those who attend singles groups vary by definition. The definition of "single" in my book is "never been married." Whereas a lot of people today will define singles as "never been married or those who have been divorced or widowed." A divorced person does not have the same struggles as I do. We are looking at singleness from two different angles. I cannot relate to a divorced woman as I can relate to a single woman according to my definition. In order to encourage and exhort and uplift, it helps more if it comes from someone who knows where you are at and where you have been. I'm not saying it is completely hopeless to minister to someone whose circumstances are not exactly like yours, it's just different. God is the one who gives the counsel and words anyway. Does this make sense?

Everyone is important to God. No one is ever overlooked or neglected by Him. That is as it should be among believers. The singles are just as important as the married. God is no respecter of persons, nor should we be. And because of their importance to God, I think it's important to point out that each one of them has a special role in the body of Christ. Just as your foot can't do without your toes, the married cannot do without the singles and the singles cannot do without the married. The young cannot do without the old and the old cannot do without the young. We all need each other. "For as we have many members in one body, and all members have not have the same office, so we, being many, are one body in Christ, and every one members one of another." (Rom. 12:4 KJV)

So, what's the single's role in the church? Glad you asked. First of all, let's make sure we are on the same page in understanding that the focus of the single woman is how she can please the Lord (have you heard this before!?). "…The unmarried woman careth about the things of the Lord, that she may be holy both in body and in spirit…." (1 Cor. 7:34 KJV)

Her focus should always be on serving the Lord and others and not on herself.

So what does a single do? In a nutshell, a single woman should do those things that the married can't. When the job calls for a single, that is your signal to act. God will direct you to what, when and where, but it is up to you to obey, go and do.

In the last several years, there have been needs that have come to my attention that could be labeled as a "Single's Job". As I talked about in the chapter "Sending Out An SOS", you can see that many of the things I have done since graduation were jobs for a single. There is no doubt a married person could have done them if there was no other way, but it would have put a lot of strain on them and their families. God gave me the opportunity and I took it.

What, when and where...
Obey, go and do.

I direct a drama club for a group of kids from church. Sometimes when we have our practices I will pick some of them up from their house and take them home again when we're through. I can remember their mom once asking me if I was sure it was okay. She hated for me to drive all the way up to the mountains and then back again. In my mind though, driving them to and from was something I could do easily because I am single. There is only one of me and there are eight of them. This is a Single's Job and I am more than glad to do it – and enjoy it immensely.

Having said all of that, be encouraged and know that you are a vital part of the body of Christ. And let's all remember to make a place in our church gathering for those people from planet earth called "Single." If the church is having a family night get-together, be sure to include the singles, every one of them is part of someone's family. If your church is ministering at the local nursing home or having a singing service with another church, see if any of the singles want to ride with you. I know I have gone places before and wished I didn't have to go by myself. Better yet, as a single, offer to drive for the widows in church, I'm sure they don't want to go by themselves anymore than we want to go by ourselves.

Singles are not to be avoided or neglected, but accepted and included in the Body of Christ. Most people seem to remember that Paul was single, but more importantly to remember is that Jesus Himself was single. Driving down the single lane is a good thing. Driving down the married lane is a good thing. God created them both therefore they are good. So, "Be kindly affectioned one to another with brotherly love; in honour preferring one another." (Rom. 12:10 KJV) And you've heard it straight from the Old Maid's mouth! ☺

Mothers...are fulfilling the highest career in the nation.

Nancy Campbell[1]

Chapter 15

The Dying Breed

On one of those many occasions when someone asked me what it was I was going to do after high school, I received the most remarkable response to my declaration, "I just want to be a homemaker." The girl I was talking with was a couple years older than I was. She was also single. Her response? "We're a dying breed aren't we?"

I was shocked. I had never heard such an encouraging reply and definitely not one that hit the nail on the head so beautifully. Homemakers are a dying breed in our society. Although it's the highest and most noble calling for a woman, tragically it's looked down upon by so many people today. If people really thought about it, they would see that there is nothing weak or degrading about it. Just about any woman can give birth to a baby, but it takes great courage, devotion and sacrificial love to be a mother.

The Proverbs 31 Woman was a homemaker and what does Proverbs 31 verse 29 say? "Many daughters have done virtuously [some versions say "nobly"], but thou excellest [or surpass] them all." (KJV) It doesn't get any better than that. Why? Because God said so. Titus 2:3-5 commands the older women to teach the younger women to "…love their husbands, to love their children, to be discreet, chaste, keepers at home, good, obedient to their own husbands…." (KJV) If God gives you the gift of marriage and blesses you with children, than you are also called to be a mother and that is a high honor indeed.

"…Come to her the highest and holiest joy known to mankind…"

President Theodore Roosevelt said, "The woman's task is not easy – no task worth doing is easy – but in doing it, and when she has done it, there shall come to her the highest and holiest joy known to mankind; and having done it, she shall have the rewards prophesied in Scripture, for her husband and children, yes, and all people who realize that her work lies at the foundation of all national happiness and greatness, shall rise up and call her blessed." We all need to realize the importance of such a calling.

Someone once said, "He who rocks the cradle, rocks the world." A mother is raising up Godly leaders for the future generation that can go out and impact the world for Jesus Christ. Without Godly leaders, our nation and ultimately the world will suffer. It has. It is. This job is so important that if mothers ceased to exist, the world would utterly fall apart. We see that happening more and more today as mothers resign their roles to others. No one else can be a mother except a mother. They are irreplaceable! And if we don't rally around these awesome women we call mothers, holding them in high esteem and supporting them in their job, our world will continue to suffer the consequences. Mothers are the legs a nation stands on. The sooner everyone realizes that, takes it to heart, responds positively to it, and acts on it the better.

History is full of men and women who have made a tremendous difference in the lives of others because of the training and raising they received by those awesome and mighty people we call mothers. Let's make the future full of such people as well.

Andrew Jackson, seventh President of the United States, said this about his mother: "There never was a woman like her. She was gentle as a dove and brave as a lioness.... The memory of my mother and her teachings were, after all the only capital I had to start life with, and on that capital I have made my way."

A mother's ministry is ministering and raising up her children for the Lord Jesus Christ. Her influence is so great, so awesome and so incredible; it has a life long effect on her children. And whether that influence is good or bad, that will depend on the mother. True mothers are awesome! And you've heard it straight from the Old Maid's mouth who doesn't know what she would do without that 5'2" tall woman she calls "Mama!" ☺

[1] Nancy Campbell is Founder and Editress of *Above Rubies* magazine.

My job is to take care
of the possible and
trust God with the impossible.

Ruth Bell Graham

Chapter 16

Becoming A Woman

Since this book is written to young women, I am quite certain that everyone who reads this will have at one time (at the very least) in their life have dreamed of meeting and falling in love with Mr. Right. <sigh> Oh, you know the one – tall, dark and as Diana Berry says, "irresistibly handsome." But then again maybe you're the type that likes a blonde, a red head or perhaps even a bald one. Whatever your fancy, he's all that you ever wanted in a husband. His character is awesomely Christ-like, he treats his family with love and respect, and he's a diligent and hard worker. <sigh> And those are only a few of his extraordinary attributes!

Well, have you ever taken a personal inventory to see if you possess qualities that would make you Miss Right in the eyes of your Mr. Right? Ouch! Isn't it true that so much of the time we focus on finding Mr. Right and having a long list of qualifications for him that we completely neglect our own attributes. Girls are not doing the only watching. Guys are watching us to see if we possess qualities that they are looking for as well. So what kind of list do you keep for yourself? What are some things you need improvement on?

And yes, despite what we would like to believe, we all could use some help. No matter what we think in our pretty little heads, we have not arrived. And if we think we have, guess what? We need to work on pride and therefore still need more work. Oh yeah, that "S" thing gets in the way once again! (What's up with that? Can't we ever get rid of it!? What if we got a bigger and better ship? Maybe that'd work!)

And, hey, I need help too. Sometimes I feel sorry for the guy that marries me. I wonder what he could see in me to want to marry me and then wonder if he has deceived himself into thinking what he sees is true. (I told you I needed help!) We all need work. And there is hope! Rest assured, ladies, God is on the job! He will continue His work in us until it is complete. "For I am confident of this very thing, that He who began a good work in you will perfect it until the day of Jesus Christ." (Phil. 1:6) Girls, I hate to break it to you, but perfection only comes when you're dead. Even though your ol' body will be six feet under, the problems and sin of this world will not be above you! The real you will be in Heaven with the Lord and "I can only imagine what that will be like". (Mercy Me)

Expecting perfection in others is a waste of good time and energy. We must instead put our energy and efforts into becoming Christ-like ourselves. "Why do you look at the speck that is in your brother's eye, but do not notice the log that is in your own eye?" (Matt. 7:3) Elisabeth Elliot puts it this way: "You will be less likely to turn into a nagging wife if you recall continually that it is not only your husband who leaves undone those things which (you think) he ought to do, and does things which (you think) he ought not to do, but that you, too, have erred and strayed like lost sheep, sinning daily by omission and commission." In our single state, we will not turn into a nagging anyone if we put this advice into practice!

Becoming Miss Right is the most important thing we could ever do. Besides, if we really think about it, *finding* Mr. Right is not our job anyway. (No sticks, no church lists, so leave that big yellow phone book alone!) God will *bring* Mr. Right in God's perfect timing.

What qualities do you possess that would be attractive to a Godly man? What weaknesses do you have that are not so attractive? But more importantly, what qualities do you possess that would be pleasing in God's sight and what areas of your life do you have that are not pleasing to Him? Where do you need to improve to become the woman God wants you to be? Are you a woman by God's definition?

You see the real issue here should be becoming who God wants us to be and not getting good enough to catch a man. It is in becoming whom God wants us to be that we should be concerned about. We should strive to become more Christ-like because God wants us to. If He brings Mr. Right along at some point in the process, then that's just an added bonus. Becoming a woman of God must come while we're still in the single lane.

Kenneth G. Smith said, "A woman is not born a woman. Nor does she become one when she marries a man, bears a child and does their dirty linen, not even when she joins a women's liberation movement. A woman becomes a woman when she becomes what God wants her to be." So open your Bible, break out the paper and pencil and get started. Ladies, it is time for a Godly check-up. And this is just a start.

We could sum up the situation with one question - In what areas of my life do I need to become more Christ-like? But let's dig deeper. Ask the Lord to reveal to you areas needing attention. Then ask Him to help you work on those things through His strength and direction to become the woman He wants you to be.

Am I a Godly woman? In other words, am I sold out for Jesus Christ? "Charm is deceitful and beauty is vain, But a woman who fears the LORD, she shall be praised." (Pro. 31:30)

Do I seek Him with my whole heart? "Now set your heart and your soul to seek the LORD your God." (1 Chron. 22:19)

Do I desire to serve Him with such a passion that nothing else takes His place in my life? "You shall have no other gods before Me." (Ex. 20:3) "…Let us have grace, whereby we may serve God acceptably with reverence and godly fear." (Heb. 12:28)

Do I strive to live my life in holiness and righteousness and in such a way that He will be honored and glorified by my example of what it means to be a Christian? "But as he which hath called you is holy, so be ye holy in all manner of conversation; Because it is written, 'Be ye holy; for I am holy.'" (1 Pet. 1:15-16 KJV) "And this I pray, that your love may abound still more and more in real knowledge and all discernment, so that you may approve the things that are excellent, in order to be sincere and blameless until the day of Christ; having been filled with the fruit of righteousness which comes through Jesus Christ, to the glory and praise of God." (Phil. 1:9-11)

Do I live totally and completely for Him? Is He first in my life? Is He my everything? My all? Or do I live for me? "I know your deeds, that you are neither cold nor hot; I would that you were cold or hot. So because you are lukewarm, and neither hot nor cold, I will spit you out of My mouth." (Rev. 3:15-16)

Am I a woman who knows the importance of prayer and puts it into practice? "The effectual fervent prayer of a righteous man availeth much." (James 5:16b KJV)

Am I a gracious, pleasant, kindhearted woman? "A gracious woman attains honor, and violent men attain riches." (Pro. 11:16)

Do I have a critical spirit? "But avoid worldly and empty chatter, for it will lead to further ungodliness, and their talk will spread like gangrene." (2 Tim. 2:16, 17a)

Is what comes out of that little yet great member of my body fit to be spoken? "A word fitly spoken is like apples of gold In pictures of silver." (Pro. 25:11 KJV) "But the tongue can no man tame; it is an unruly evil, full of deadly poison. Therewith bless we God, even the Father; and therewith curse we men, which are made after the similitude of God. Out of the same mouth proceedeth blessing and cursing. My brethren, these things ought not so to be." (James 3:8-10 KJV)

Am I a servant? First to God, then my family and others, thinking more of them and less of myself? "Do nothing from selfishness or empty conceit, but with humility of mind let each of you regard one another as more important than himself; do not merely look out for your own personal interests, but also for the interests of others." (Phil. 2:3-4)

Do I show love to all? Do I know what love really is? "Love is patient, love is kind, and is not jealous; love does not brag and is not arrogant, does not act unbecomingly; it does not seek its own, is not provoked, does not take into account a wrong suffered, does not rejoice in unrighteousness, but rejoices with the truth; bears all things, believes all things, hopes all things, endures all things. Love never fails;" (1 Cor. 13:4-8) And remember… "Let us not love with word or with tongue, but in deed and truth." (1 John 3:18)

Do I have the qualities of the Titus 2 Woman? "Older women likewise are to be reverent in their behavior, not malicious gossips, nor enslaved to much wine, teaching what is good, that they may encourage the young women to love their husbands, to love their children, to be sensible, pure, workers at home, kind, being subject to their own husbands, that the word of God may not be dishonored." (Titus 2:3-5)

Do I have a burden for the souls of others, desiring to win them to Christ? "And Jesus came up and spoke to them, saying, 'All authority has been given to Me in heaven and on earth. Go therefore and make disciples of all the nations, baptizing them in the name of the Father and the Son and the Holy Spirit, teaching them to observe all that I commanded you; and lo, I am with you always, even to the end of the age.'" (Matt. 28:18-20)

Do I have the desire to fulfill the commandment to be hospitable? “Be hospitable to one another without complaint.” (1 Pet. 4:9)

Am I reverent, honorable, honest, not a slanderer, temperate, faithful in all things? These are the attributes of a bishop’s wife, which we would do well to imitate. “Women must likewise be dignified, not malicious gossips, but temperate, faithful in all things.” (1 Tim. 3:11)

Am I a wise woman or a foolish woman? “The wise woman builds her house, But the foolish tears it down with her own hands.” (Pro. 14:1)

Am I a Proverbs 31 Woman? Am I virtuous? Can I be trusted? Do I do others good and not evil? Do I work willingly with my hands? Do I consider the poor and help them? Is strength and honor my clothing? Do I open my mouth with wisdom and in my tongue is the law of kindness? Do I eat the bread of idleness? Can God say that many daughters have done virtuously, but I excel them all? The Proverbs 31 Woman is quite the model for each of us. I highly recommend reading the book entitled, *Beautiful in God’s Eyes* by Elizabeth George. She does a wonderful job of looking in-depth at this remarkable woman. And even though you may feel like you will never be able to hold a candle to her, remember that we can do all things through Jesus Christ who gives us the strength. “Who can find a virtuous wife? for her worth is far above rubies.” (Pro. 31:10 KJV)

And last but not least, am I content where God has placed me at this time in my life or do I continue to do battle with that “C” thing? While visiting with my friend and her beau (who later became her husband), he said something I will never forget. He told me that a man doesn’t want a wife that doesn’t know how to be content because if she’s not content while she’s single, than she won’t be content when she’s married

The list could go on and on, but do not be discouraged! I know how pitiful you feel when you take a spiritual inventory of your life – I have been there, done that and continue to do so! But the good news is God is faithful! God will complete His perfect work in our lives. (Have I said that enough yet or do I need to say it again!?) He never gives up on us and He never leaves us on our own to keep our heads above water. God is faithful, ladies! God is good! God loves us! God takes us and turns us into something beautiful for Him, if we allow Him to do His work in us. Most of the time it is a painful process, but it’ll be worth it in the end. God said it. Believe it.

I am praying for each of you. I may not know you, but God does. God sees, hears, and God answers. So be encouraged! Remember, you’ve heard it straight from the Old Maid’s mouth who needs God to continue His perfect work in her life that she too may become the woman God wants her to be! ☺

Help, Lord,

for the godly man ceases to be!

Psalm 12:1

Chapter 17

Setting Your Sights High

Okay, now that we have established a list of qualifications for ourselves, let's look at what we are looking for in our Mr. Right – or as Pastor David Crispin says, "Mr. Junior Right, because God is Mr. Right." But first, I want to pass on to you the most encouraging thing anyone has ever said to me. A young married mother of two precious little girls and another on the way said, "Don't let anyone tell you you're too picky. Hello! This is the man you're gonna marry!" She told me your children will act just like him, so consider that when considering him.

Let's think seriously about this. This is the second most important decision of your life (choosing salvation being the first) therefore it is absolutely, positively, without question, controversy or doubt, acceptable to be picky! Girls, setting your sights high is OKAY. Someone once said, "It's better to be single than to wish you were." Don't settle for less than God's absolute best for you! You will never regret it – guaranteed. Don't let anything – especially those years that continue to fly by in rapid succession - cause you to lower your standards. Just because you're not married at this moment, does not mean you lower the standards for yourself. Does God ever lower His standards for us because of circumstances? Never! Don't give up! We don't need to fear and question, "Can God really bring a Godly man for me?" God shall supply all your need. Nothing is impossible for God! Believe me, if God has someone for you, He will bring him eventually – in God's timing, not yours and not the guy's. So set your standards and don't back down!

However, there's a "Caution" sign beside the roadway. If you are anything like me, you know exactly how it is. You tell yourself and even others encourage you to "set your sights high and don't settle for anything less than God's absolute best for you." And you believe it and claim it. But then somehow that wears off and you subconsciously lower not your standards, but your faith and expectations for what God can do. Why is it that I sometimes tend to doubt that even a guy so awesome and wonderful and Godly as I desire even exists, when God is the One at the helm directing this beautiful and romantic love story? You and I don't need to worry about ANYTHING. We don't need to worry about how God is going to bring the right one around or what we're suppose to say when this guy shows his interest or all those other things that tend to run through our pretty little heads. When I allow Aprill to get into such a tizzy, I am not trusting God to bring me the right one who does have all the right qualifications. God has a plan, so why do I doubt His ability to carry out that plan so awesomely and beautifully as only He can? Just call me doubting Thomasita because my faith is not always as it should be. God is so awesome and nothing is too hard for Him, but sometimes I forget just how great He is. My prayer should be, "Forgive me, Lord, for doubting your incredible power. I put You in a box way too often. Help me to step aside so You can step forward." Isn't it comforting to know that when God has my life in His capable hands, I really have no need, and I should have no want, to worry about any of it? God already knows each and every one of my fears - getting to truly know this guy, him getting to know the real me, becoming best friends, et cetera, et cetera. Our awesome Savior can take care of each fear with no trouble. So stop worrying, my friends! With God, it's going to be okay.

All right, now that we've established that God is fully capable and ready for anything and that we *should* be picky, let's break out the guy's list. What exactly does this awesome guy look like? To sum it up, Mr. Junior Right is to be a man of Godly character and integrity, mature both in the Lord and otherwise. We must make God the foundation of our relationship and the focus of our devotion. Come on, let's dig!

I received a teaching one time about what to look for in a husband. Pastor Fraley suggested using the guidelines for a bishop as outlined in 1 Timothy 3:2-7.

"A bishop then must be blameless, the husband of one wife, vigilant, sober, of good behaviour, given to hospitality, apt to teach; Not given to wine, no striker, not greedy of filthy lucre; but patient, not a brawler, not covetous; One that ruleth well his own house, having his children in subjection with all gravity; (For if a man know not how to rule his own house, how shall he take care of the church of God?) Not a novice, lest being lifted up with pride he fall into the condemnation of the devil. Moreover he must have a good report of them which are without; lest he fall into reproach and the snare of the devil." (1 Tim. 3:2-7)

So, Mr. Junior Right needs to have the following qualities:

1.) Blameless (or without rebuke, i.e. a David – even though he sinned and fell short, he admitted his wrong to God and those he sinned against; a man after God's own heart; how easily does he admit he's wrong?)

2.) One-woman Man, as Pastor Fraley says (not a flirt)

3.) Alert (vigilant, temperate, composed)

4.) Sober-minded (self-controlled; Pastor Fraley says not a jokester all the time, but can have fun)

5.) Good manners (ah yes! a gentleman; but remember, in order for him to treat you like a lady, you must first act like one!)

6.) Hospitable (invests in the lives of others)

7.) Able to teach (knows what he believes and is able to communicate it to others)

8.) Not given to wine (self-explanatory I think!)

9.) Not violent (to anyone)

10.) Not greedy for money (once again self-explanatory; however, it does imply he works to make some money – the guy must have a job!)

11.) Gentle (patient, kind, tender)

12.) Doesn't argue ("It is honorable for a man to stop striving, Since any fool can start a quarrel." Pro. 20:3)

13.) Not covetous (is content with what God has given him)

14.) Manages his household well (Pastor Fraley said to determine how he does on this one, look at how he takes care of his vehicle! Another way we could look at this is, how well does he manage his money)

15.) Not a novice (new convert to Jesus Christ – how can a baby lead his family?)

16.) Have a good testimony (he must be a man of good reputation or honest report full of the Holy Spirit and wisdom, just like the men in Acts 6:3 who were to be considered in taking Judas Iscariot's place. "Therefore, brethren, seek out from among you seven men of good reputation, full of the Holy Spirit and wisdom…")

We could take our own list and use some of it as a quality checklist for him as well. Is he a Godly man sold out for Jesus? Does he serve God with a passion and desire to do His will in everything above what his own desires may be? Does he seek Him with his whole heart? Does he strive to live his life in holiness and righteousness bringing glory and honor to God? Is he a man of prayer and faith? What comes out of his mouth – words that lift up or ones that tear down? Is he a good listener? Does he communicate well?

And one quality that I think deserves extra special recognition is that of a leader. Is he a leader, not a dictator or tyrant? Can he be the head of his home? "For the husband is the head of the wife, as Christ also is the head of the church, He Himself being the Savior of the body." (Eph. 5:23) What a role model for the man – Jesus Christ! But more importantly, is this man a *servant* leader? Let's take a moment to look at the phrase "servant leader," it's not one we hear about very often.

First of all, the man in question needs to be a servant – did not even Jesus come to serve and not to be served? "Just as the Son of Man did not come to be served, but to serve, and to give His life a ransom for many." (Matt. 20:28) If any one deserves to be waited on hand and foot it is the Son of the Living God! But instead, Jesus washed the dirty, stinky feet of His disciples (remember, these guys only wore sandals and walked on dirt roads all the time! Pew!). Jesus served others through love – 1 Corinthians 13 love. We are called to do the same. "For you were called to freedom, brethren; only do not turn your freedom into an opportunity for the flesh, but through love serve one another." (Gal. 5:13) Paul likens the way a man is to treat his wife as Christ treats His church – "Husbands, love your wives, just as Christ also loved the church and gave Himself up for her…For no one ever hated his own flesh, but nourishes and cherishes it, just as Christ also does the church." (Eph. 5:25 and 29) Jesus loved so much, Jesus served so much, He gave His very life. A servant must first think of others and himself last.

Okay, but not only was Jesus a servant, He was a leader. He was called "Master" and "Teacher". Matthew 7:21 says He taught as one having authority. There is example after example of Jesus being a leader – the Bible is full! But He didn't lord it over anyone – "But Jesus called them to Himself, and said, 'You know that the rulers of the Gentiles lord it over them, and their great men exercise authority over them. It is not so among you, but whoever wishes to become great among you shall be your servant, and whoever wishes to be first among you shall be your slave; just as the Son of Man did not come to be served, but to serve, and to give His life a ransom for many." (Matt. 20:25-28) Jesus was both a servant and a leader – the best example, of what honestly seems like an incomprehensible paradox, that we will ever have! Jimmy Evans says, "A servant's heart is the most important quality in leadership." And, ladies, it is okay to set our sights high in wanting a man who is Christ-like!

"A servant's heart is the most important quality in leadership."

Jesus also loved, I mean really loved. He loved so much that He was willing to leave the comforts of Heaven to be born a man and die for the sins of others. "Greater love has no one than this, that one lay down his life for his friends." (John 15:13) How does our Mr. Junior Right demonstrate such awesome sacrifice for others?

I have also heard it said to notice how he treats his mother – with honor and respect or dishonor and disrespect? He will treat his wife the same way. The same goes for how a daughter treats her dad and how she will treat her husband.

Remember! We are not looking for perfection here! You will never find a perfect man or woman no matter how long you look! But we are looking for a man after God's own heart. We are looking for the cream of the crop, not watered down 2%! We want the real thing! (And that's OKAY!!!)

So allow me to say it again – do not settle for less than God's absolute best – God's ideal for you! Be picky – it effects the rest of your life, the lives of your children, grandchildren, great-grandchildren, great great-grandchildren…you get the idea! What you see is what you get. There is no changing him after the fact, just as he can't change you.

"But a faithful man who can find?" (Pro. 20:6b KJV) I have wondered this very thing, but God has allowed me to meet some men (who are not related) that are diligently seeking to do His will. So, yes, absolutely there are Godly men out there! God is raising up Godly men and Godly women – He is only waiting on His perfect timing to bring them together for His glory!

And, yes, you've heard it straight from the Old Maid's mouth who has seen the faithfulness of God! ☺

Nothing beats
love at first sight
except love with insight.

Unknown

Chapter 18

Thinking Ahead

Author of the book entitled *Marriage on the Rock*, Jimmy Evans points out something quite astounding. "Society requires years of preparation for almost any significant career endeavor, but demands no real preparation for one of the most crucial undertakings in life: marriage." How true that is!

As my mother has said, many people view marriage as this great event in their lives, one so big and so grand, that just getting there is what they are consumed with. It would probably be more appropriate to say they pour more effort, time and energy into the "wedding" than they do their marriage. It's like all they see is the "wedding" and no one ever thinks to look beyond the grand event. After the ceremony is over, the cake has been cut and eaten, and the guests have left, life does go on. Everyday life is waiting on the other side of the threshold. There are adjustments that need to take place and many different decisions to be made. For the man there is a marriage to work on, a wife and family to lead and to provide for, a secure home to provide, a job to go to every day, dealings with the in-laws and out-laws – the list is endless. For the wife there is a husband to stand with, a marriage to work on, children to care for (not immediate, but it will come), a home to run, and dealings with his side of the family and her side – the list is endless.

Thinking about what will come after the ceremony even before beginning a relationship is truly preparing for marriage. The wedding marks an end but also a beginning – the end of singleness, the beginning of your marriage with your husband. The wedding (whether it's small or large) is simply the means of getting you married. So let's look beyond the variety of flowers, the style of dresses and the color of napkins! It's time to think ahead!

Okay, so what if the Lord does send a guy along? (I am going to call him a "guy" even though we are looking for a man - not a boy and not someone who is simply male. We want a man.) What is your role in the whole process? What kinds of things are important to you that need to be important to him as well? What things do you need to agree on and what things can you agree to disagree? What is important enough to be a "must" agree upon and what is not so important? (And even though this is an old maid talking, I have watched others who have been down this road and I've taken notes! Now, it's not to say I know everything, because that is down right hilarious – I do NOT know everything!)

First of all, the most important issue that should head the top of the list is that of the guy's salvation. He must be a born again, blood bought, Spirit taught believer. God says, "Be ye not unequally yoked together with unbelievers: for what fellowship hath righteousness with unrighteousness? and what communion hath light with darkness?" (2 Cor. 6:14 KJV) Period. I bring this up because I feel very strongly about this issue and because God feels strongly about it. He wants only your best, and marriage to an unbeliever is not in your best interest.

"But wait a minute! You don't understand," some may say, "we love each other. We both are committed to making this marriage work. We will do whatever it takes, no matter how long it takes, no matter the cost! We will make it work! We can do this. We are here for the duration." Sound convincing enough? No doubt such a person is very sincere and truly believes that they can make marriage to an unbeliever work.

But God is not so easily convinced. God knows it will never work.

Let me ask you, can oil and water mix? Let's just say for a moment that you decide to make it into the Genus World Book of Records as the first person to ever successfully mix oil and water. You are dedicated, sincere, and committed to the cause. You measure out equal amounts of oil and water and put them into a jar. You seal the lid with a flourish and so begin your endeavor. You shake vigorously at first, determined that your plan will work if you only put your whole heart into it. As you tire somewhat, you remember your objective and press on reminding yourself of the commitment you made to see this through. After a while you stop shaking to see the progress. As you watch, the oil and water begin to separate. The longer you watch the greater your disappointment becomes. It didn't work. However, you set your jaw, pick up the jar once again and begin to shake. All day you do the same thing – shake, stop, shake, stop. By the end of the day, your devotion has wanned somewhat. Thinking that perhaps if you let the two just sit for a while getting used to each other, things will look brighter in the morning. The next day you awaken refreshed, renewed and quite anxious to get to your project. Much to your dismay, however, as the day wears on, it becomes clear that all the devotion, all the commitment, all the work in the world does not help. You could try and try to mix oil and water together until dooms day but you never can do it. It is not possible. That is just the way it is. It will not work.

The same is true when trying to mix an unbeliever and a believer in a marriage. Oil and water do not mix. Light and darkness do not mix. The unbeliever and believer do not mix. God says, "Be ye not unequally yoked together with unbelievers," and that includes marriage to an unbeliever. Girls, marriage to an unbeliever is NOT an option. This issue is nonnegotiable. Non-debatable. Period. God said so. And He said so for your best. So don't even let the possibility of marrying someone who is not saved enter your mind. "Well if so and so got saved then we could get married…" Don't even go there! It is for your own good that God has given this commandment. Remember He desires the very best for His daughter – you – and when God does something, it is awesome!

Okay now that we are considering a believer, it is important for us to realize that the number one reason to get married is companionship. In the beginning God said, "'It is not good for the man to be alone; I will make him a helper suitable for him.'…So the LORD God caused a deep sleep to fall upon the man, and he slept; then He took one of his ribs, and closed up the flesh at that place. And the LORD God fashioned into a woman the rib which He had taken from the man, and brought her to the man. And the man said, 'This is now bone of my bones, And flesh of my flesh; She shall be called Woman, Because she was taken out of Man.' For this cause a man shall leave his father and his mother, and shall cleave to his wife; and they shall become one flesh." (Genesis 2:18, 21-24) I am sure that none of us will have a problem with agreeing about this one – we don't exactly get overjoyed at the prospect of being alone.

Number Two. You should only get married if you can serve God better together than if you both remain single. Since the number one reason for our existence is to have a relationship with Jesus Christ and serve Him, it only makes sense that we keep that as our number one goal no matter what we are doing or where we are. So our number one goal as a couple – husband and wife – should be to maintain that relationship with the Lord and serve Him with our everything. "I am crucified with Christ: nevertheless I live; yet not I, but Christ liveth in me: and the life which I now live in the flesh I live by the faith of the Son of God, who loved me, and gave himself for me." (Gal. 2:20 KJV)

Keep the number one goal #1 in every season of your life.

The third important reason for getting married is children. We need to realize that God designed marriage for the raising up of Godly seed (Malachi 2:15). A lot of times this fact is overlooked or swept under the carpet. However, God said it. Believe it. If you or the guy don't want children (for whatever reason), I strongly suggest you take a closer look at why you are getting married. If God says something, the matter is non-negotiable. If God said it, He meant it. Listen to what God told man in the beginning: "And God created man in His own image, in the image of God He created him; male and female He created them. And God blessed them; and God said to them, "Be fruitful and multiply, and fill the earth, and subdue it…" (Gen. 1:27-28a)

Some women are not physically able to have children (and I mean due to something in their make up, not by their own means). If this is the case, God is the one in control, not woman or man. Look at Sarah, Rachel and Hannah – God was the one who shut their wombs AND opened them, not Sarah, not Rachel, not Hannah. We need to be pure in our motives for marriage. When we leave it up to God when and how many children to give us, then God is the one in control. God is the giver of life, not us. So if a couple has given this issue into God's care, it is God who opens or closes the womb.

Having said that, in my estimation, it is a good idea to know what you believe and what is important to you before any guy comes along. If you have things mapped out in your own mind, then it makes it a whole lot easier. For instance, is it important to you to celebrate Christmas? Birthdays? Thanksgiving? If it is important to you but not him, then you're not compatible. If you don't have any conviction one way or the other and he does, then you can go along with his conviction and be totally okay with that. What do I mean?

What things do you have to agree on and what is not important? For instance, something that is very important to me is children. My husband and I have to agree that marriage is designed for producing Godly seed as God says in Malachi 2:15. We also have to agree that children are a blessing (Psalm 127) and that God is in control of when we have children and how many we have. God is the Giver of Life, is in control of every situation, He knows what's best, and He knows what we can handle through His strength. "Behold, children are a heritage from the LORD, The fruit of the womb is a reward." (Psalm 127:3) We have to agree about birth control. I don't believe in any form of birth control and it's not an option for me to use it at any point in time. I feel very strongly about this, therefore it is high on my list of "Musts". The "guy" must believe the same way.

Now Christmas trees are a different matter. I don't feel anything one way or the other. If he thinks we should/can, then I'll go along with that. If he doesn't, then that's fine too. See the difference?

What is important enough to agree upon? Get those issues out in the open at once. Honesty and being open from the beginning is vital. Don't let your relationship go on and on and then all of a sudden drop a bombshell on the guy. Of course, I'm sure no one wants to do that deliberately, some things just kind of sneak up on you. That is why it is a good idea to think of all the things that are important to you ahead of time so you don't get down the road and then realize you missed something. Do not *assume* anything. Talk about *everything*.

To organize your thoughts, make a list of the issues that are important enough to you that you and your potential mate have to agree upon in order to be compatible. For example, what are your beliefs about…

God – how important is it that He be the center of your lives and the center of your marriage

Bible – is it the infallible Word of God or not

Jesus – who is He; is He the Son of God

Holy Spirit – is He part of the Trinity

Salvation – saved by grace through faith by the blood of Jesus; can you lose it

Children – marriage is for raising up Godly seed, the question is when and how many; will you use birth control; what does God say

Abortion – is it ever an option (I pray to God the answer is no); what if one of your unborn children have some sort of deformity

Holidays – which ones you celebrate and those you don't; (it won't hurt to talk about whose family will you spending which holiday with)

Television/Movies – what's your standard; will you even own a TV

Baptism – infant and adult; sprinkling or immersion; is it what saves you

Ministry – full time or part time; does he have a vision for what God is calling him and his wife to do

Attending church – how high of a priority is it in your life/in his; what kind of church to attend

Hospitality – do you like to have people over; is it a command given in Scripture

Tithing – 10% on everything you receive; is it the first thing you give or do bills come first

Winning souls – how high of a priority is it

Prayer and reading the Bible – will there be a time you do it together

Child training – do you or don't you feel your children should be instructed with the board of education (spanked); what about time out

Child birth – at home or hospital; will you use a bottle or nurse

Education for the children – home school, public, private, college

Working outside the home – what's your thoughts on
wives/mothers working
Debt – should you ever go into debt

Some of these things (and this list is not complete, you get to do that) may seem crazy to you and some may not. That's the idea. What do you believe and how important is it to you. Notice I didn't say, "What does your family believe?" You are the one marrying this guy and the you will live with him for the rest of your life. Your parents or siblings won't have to live with him for the rest of their lives. You and him have to agree. Remember to see what God says about each of these issues first. God should be the standard we use for every part of our lives.

God should be the standard we use for every part of our lives.

Getting issues settled on before you say "I do" is so much better than having to deal with them after the honeymoon (and perhaps even on the honeymoon). And you are not the only one effected by your choice in mate. You will not only live with your decision for the rest of your life, but so will your children. You can afford to be cautious. Don't rush it. It's okay to take as much time as you need to make the second most important decision of your life.

And don't ever underestimate the advantage of having a multitude of counselors. "Where no counsel is, the people fall; But in the multitude of counselors *there* is safety." (Pro. 11:14 KJV) I have a list of people who I know hear from God, who know me, and whom I greatly respect, that I want to be apart of every step of the relationship. And it is a given that my parents are at the top of that list. I believe that through the Holy Spirit, every one on the list can be in agreement one hundred percent. And if any one of them is not at peace with me marrying the potential husband, we don't move forward until they are or we don't get married at all. And I don't go find another counselor who will agree with me either. God has to be the center and in control. There is no doubt in my mind that He can bring everyone into agreement with His perfect will. There is safety in a multitude of counselors.

"In the multitude of counselors there is safety."

Now, let's not forget that just believing alike is not enough. There may be guys that I agree on things about but that doesn't mean they are the "one" for me. Agreeing on doctrine and standards is not the tell-tell sign. Thinking ahead is only a small part in the big picture, but it is a very important part.

I pray this gives you something to think about and meditate on. One of the advantages of still being single is that you have the opportunity to start your marriage on the right foot. The more issues you deal with before marriage, the less you have to deal with after marriage. Nothing is smooth sailing in this world, but at least getting a jump-start makes the ride a little more pleasant. And, yes, you've heard it straight from the Old Maid's mouth! ☺

Let marriage be held in honor among all, and let the marriage bed be undefiled...

Hebrews 13:4

Chapter 19

Purity No Matter the Cost

I don't think any book written to single women would be complete without some word spoken about the importance of staying pure before marriage.

Virginity is another gift given by God. This gift is so special and so unique it's like no other gift. In fact, each of us is only given this treasure once in our entire lives. Treasure it and protect it at all costs. I know without a doubt that it will be worth the wait. Why? Because God designed sex for marriage and if it's God's idea and unique creation to save yourself for marriage, then it's got to be good. Remember that everything God does is for the best, so I don't think that we're being shortchanged or missing out on something because God wants us to wait. He is not withholding a pleasure from us like some sinister tyrant. He knows that when we give ourselves away to someone who is not our husband, we are opening up ourselves to a lot of pain, hurt, and possible disease. Notice that I didn't mention pregnancy. It's not because you won't get pregnant because it only takes one time to create a baby. No, you can live through a pregnancy, what you might not live through is a sexually transmitted disease (STD). Most people think that getting pregnant is the worst thing that can happen to you, but it's not. Having to live with an incurable disease for the rest of your life is horrendous, but death is even more hideous and definitely has a more permanent effect on your life. That may sound like a play on words, but the end result of many STDs is drastic. More and more people are becoming infected with Chlamydia, Herpes, Gonorrhea, Syphilis, AIDS, Hepatitis B, and Human Papilloma Virus (HPV). "One out of 5 Americans has a viral infection. Up to 1/3 of all sexually active teens are infected with Chlamydia, a disease that can cause infertility. HPV causes over 93 percent of all cervical cancer." (Albuquerque Pregnancy Center) Every one of these diseases is ugly and has life long effects, even deadly ones. It's not worth the risk.

Some may rationalize that everyone is doing it so what's the point. Why wait? But everyone isn't doing it. I'm not and I know many other young women who are saving themselves for the one God has for them too. That means everyone is not doing it. If even one person in a crowd of people is not doing it, then that means not everyone is. It may be a struggle and it may be hard to stand up and be the odd one in the group, but believe me, when you do things the way God designed you will receive blessings in abundance. Great will be your reward. And not only that, you'll like yourself, accept yourself and be able to respect yourself a whole lot more.

Some may think it's out of date or old fashion to save yourself for the man you marry much less for your wedding night, but let me assure you it's not. I had a friend tell me one time that she thought the whole honeymoon thing was made to be something more than it should be. She said everyone sleeps with each other before they're married anyway so what's the big deal about a honeymoon. Some couples who have had premarital sex say that sex is so different after the wedding and honeymoon than before. "I'm sorry," my friend told me indignantly, "it's not any different." Once you've opened the package, it's never the same.

Dear girls, "Flee immorality. Every other sin that a man commits is outside the body, but the immoral man sins against his own body. Or do you not know that your body is a temple of the Holy Spirit who is in you, whom you have from God, and that you are not your own? For you have been bought with a price: therefore glorify God in your body." (1 Cor. 6:18-20)

"For by Him [Jesus] ... All things were created by Him, and for Him." (Col. 1:16 KJV) "All things" includes our bodies. Pastor Justin Crispin says, "Our bodies were created by God, for God, to honor God."

Jesus said, "But from the beginning of the creation, God 'made them male and female. For this reason a man shall leave his father and mother and cleave to his wife, and they twain shall be one flesh'; so then they are no more twain, but one flesh. What therefore God hath joined together, let not man put asunder." (Mark 10:6-9 KJV)

Have you ever read about the Proverbs 31 Woman? No doubt you have, but have you ever noticed what verses 11 and 12 say? "The heart of her husband doth safely trust in her, so that he shall have no need of spoil. She will do him good and not evil all the days of her life." (KJV) I have no idea how many times I have read this Scripture, but it never struck me the way it did just the other day. This woman does her husband good, not just when she is his wife, but "all" the days of her life. Wow! "All" meaning from the time she is born to the time she dies! Perhaps we could personalize this powerful verse this way: "The heart of my future husband has full confidence in me. I will do him good and not evil all the days of my life - *including* the days of my life when I don't even know who he is." Isn't that awesome!!!??? Can you say that? Can I?

We need to ask ourselves, "By doing such and such or acting thus, am I doing good or evil to my future husband?" Be faithful in the heart and in the physical before you are married and you will set the pattern for after you are married.

By having sex before marriage, one is doing evil to their future spouse – even if you eventually marry the person you have slept with. God's awesome grace and infinite strength will sustain us through every temptation. For every temptation, there is a way of escape (1 Cor. 10:13). God never leaves us. Be watchful that you don't fall in your strength, confidence or pride. NEVER let your guard down.

If you have unwrapped the gift of your virginity and given it away to a man who is not your husband, be encouraged because there is hope and healing through Jesus Christ. My friend, let me assure you that there is nothing, yes *nothing* that God's grace and forgiveness can't touch and heal. Period. 1 John 1:9 says it all. "If we confess our sins [it doesn't matter what we've done], He [Jesus] is faithful and just to forgive us our sins and to cleanse us from all unrighteousness." (KJV) Period. God said it. God promised it. Believe it. Claim that promise. You will be clean. Virginity is not something that can be taken back once given, but God "heals the brokenhearted and binds up their wounds." (Psa. 147:3) Psalm 103:12 says He removes our transgressions as far as the east is from the west. Isaiah 1:18 says God washes our sins as white as snow, though they are red like crimson. Isaiah 43:25 says God wipes out our sins and will not remember them any more. And once the slate has been washed clean, we can start afresh and do things the way God intended. It will be beautiful.

"Wash me thoroughly from mine iniquity, and cleanse me from my sin…Against Thee, Thee only, have I sinned, And done this evil in Thy sight…Purge me with hyssop, and I shall be clean; Wash me, and I shall be whiter than snow…Create in me a clean heart, O God, and renew a right spirit within me. Cast me not away from Thy presence, and do not take Thy Holy Spirit from me. Restore unto me the joy of Thy salvation, and uphold me with Thy free Spirit…The sacrifices of God are a broken spirit, A broken and a contrite heart, O God, Thou wilt not despise." (Psa. 51:2, 4, 8, 10-12, 17 KJV)

There is hope – His name is Jesus! God's grace, God's forgiveness and God's cleansing power is in great abundance just for you. Cry out to Him, pour out your heart and He will hear and answer you. He will wrap His arms around you and lovingly wipe the tears from your eyes. His love for you is great and He wants you. God says, "…Fear not; for I have redeemed thee; I have called thee by thy name; thou art mine." (Isa. 43:1 KJV) Jesus died for you and He died for me. Our slate is wiped clean because of the blood He shed in our place for our sins. And if God forgives us, girls, we need to forgive ourselves. He is faithful. His love for you is so great. He wants to make you clean. Embrace His love and forgiveness and cleansing power as your own. He will never fail you.

My friends, there are consequences to everything we do. Sin will always find us out. Play with fire and we will get burned. Sex is not something to play around with. God designed it to be enjoyed between a husband and his wife. Period. No special exclusions apply to anyone and there are no excuses or rationalizations that can change His perfect design. He created it this way because it is the very best. The best! Nothing gets better than God's best! Anything else, any other thinking, any other human arrangement is the exact opposite of good. Don't be fooled. God did not design sex to be shared only between a husband and wife to be mean to unmarried people and withhold something awesome and exciting from them. Remember that God loves us and wants the very BEST for us. That is true in everything He does, even sex. Trust Him. Trust Him all the way and He guarantees that you will not regret it.

I do not have even one iota of regret in giving this part of my life over to God. I know that it will be worth the wait. I wouldn't want it to be any other way, because when God does something, when God says something, it's going to be good, way awesome and way beyond what I could ever imagine. Hey, you've heard it straight from the Old Maid's mouth who is saving this awesome gift for marriage! ☺

Faithful is He
who calls you, and
He also will bring it to pass.

1 Thessalonians 5:24

Chapter 20

God's Success Rate

Has God ever failed? If we could turn back the pages of time, would we ever find a moment when God did not succeed in accomplishing His will and perfect plan? Has God ever let someone down? Has God ever not answered when someone called upon Him? Has God ever failed to be God? What is His success rate?

When facing an impossible situation, the last thing a person needs is someone who is not qualified or fit to lean upon or trust. There is an urgency to have someone we can depend on no matter what is going to happen next, no matter the duration of the problem or problems, no matter the cost and quite honestly no matter *what*. But let's face it, we all have had someone let us down in our most critical time of need. The success rate of humans varies but none of them could qualify as a perfect rating. Now God is a different story. He is in a class all of His own.

God's success rate (no matter the case or situation) is 1 in 1. God always succeeds. God never fails. God never makes a mistake. God never leaves. God never forsakes. God is faithful. God is the Alpha and the Omega. God is the Beginning and the End. God is God. He knows what is going to happen in the world and in our lives before it even thinks about starting. With God all things are possible.

God always succeeds. He never fails!

The Bible is full of God's success stories. He proves over and over again that He is worthy of our trust. Let's take a moment to look at the life of Hannah, Samuel's mother.

Wow! Now this is quite a woman. Hannah was one of the two wives of Elkanah, and even though her husband loved her, she had no children because the LORD had shut up her womb. Hannah really, really wanted children. I Samuel 1:10 (KJV) says that she was in "bitterness of soul" or as the Hebrew puts it, "discontented."

I'm sure you know the story. While she and her husband were in Shiloh for their yearly worship and sacrifice she prayed before the Lord. Eli, the priest, was nearby and saw her lips moving but no sound was made. Thinking her drunk, Eli reprimanded her. She replied, "No, my lord, I am a woman of sorrowful spirit. I have drunk neither wine nor strong drink, but have *poured out my soul before the LORD*." (I Sam. 1:15 KJV, *italics mine*) David tells us in Psalm 62:8, "Trust in Him at all times, ye people; Pour out your heart before Him; God is a refuge for us. Selah." (KJV)

Hannah trusted God enough to pour out her deepest desire to Him. She knew He was trustworthy. She knew He could handle it. So what happened? Eli tells her, "Go in peace, and may the God of Israel grant your petition that you have asked of Him." (I Sam. 1:17) In verse nineteen, it says that the Lord remembered her. God heard and God answered. In the next verse, is says she bore a son and called his name Samuel, Hannah said, "Because I have asked him of the LORD." She poured out her heart before God, asking Him for a son and God came through faithfully. David said, "He will fulfill the desire of those who fear Him; He will also hear their cry and will save them." (Psalm 145:19) Hannah is a testimony of God's success rate. We too can pour out our hearts before the Lord, entrust to Him our deepest desires and He will faithfully do what is in His perfect plan for our lives. God's success rate never fails.

Mary, the mother of Jesus, is yet another testimony of God's success rate. Her dream was to marry Joseph and have a family. However, God's plan for her life disrupted and at first glance, destroyed all her hopes and dreams. A woman in her day that was found pregnant out of wedlock was stoned to death! By following God's plan for her life, she could lose it. (Hmm, sound familiar? "He who has found his life shall lose it, and he who has lost his life for My sake shall find it." Matt. 10:39)

But what did she do? She didn't complain, balk or try to get God to see it from her point of view or even try to talk Him out of it. She said, "Behold the handmaid of the Lord! be it unto me according to Thy word." (Luke 1:38 KJV) She didn't know all that was going to happen. She only knew how she was going to conceive since she didn't know a man - the Holy Spirit would come upon her and the power of the Highest would overshadow her. She didn't know how God was going to save her from being stoned to death (for in order for all to come to pass that the angel said she would have to remain alive). She didn't know if Joseph would marry her anyway or if she would be cast from her father's house and have no place to go. She did know to trust God to give her the information she needed to know and whatever kind of provision she needed to have in order for His plan to be accomplished. He gave her every thing she needed to carry out what He had called her to do. In the same way, God will give us what we need in order to do what He has called us to do. Once again He is faithful and once again His success rate is flawless.

Now let's look at Sarah, Abraham's wife. What was God's success rate in her situation? First, what was Sarah's heart's desire? Like Hannah, she wanted a child. However, Sarah went about things a little differently than Hannah did. Sarah had her own way of doing things – her own plan – and she thought it was foolproof.

Let's get some background information of the situation first. In Genesis chapter 12, God calls Abram (God had yet to change his name to Abraham) to leave his homeland. Verse 2 God promises Abram that He will make of him a "great nation" and how can that be except he produce a son. In chapter 13, God promised Abram that his descendents would be "as the dust of the earth." Again in chapter 15 God promises him an heir, but not just any ol' heir. God specifically tells Abram that his heir would come from his own body. God also promised that his seed would be as numerous as the stars. And Abraham believed God and it was counted unto him as righteousness (Gen. 15:6).

Then comes chapter 16. Sarai (God had not changed her name to Sarah yet) went to her husband with a grand scheme - or so she thought it was - as to how they could have a son. She gave her maid, Hagar, to Abram as a wife. Hagar did conceive and bare a son Ishmael. The child was from Abram's body, but it was not part of God's perfect plan. Sarah (and Abraham as well) neglected to consult God. If He were the One who promised she would have a son, it seems reasonable to think He had a plan to make it happen. God is never unprepared so He knew what He wanted to do in their lives way before the foundations of the earth were laid! But Sarah chose her own way, her own path to follow, her own plan for her life. And how good did it turn out? Not at all! It backfired. Hagar ended up despising Sarah, and Abram had to send both her and his son Ishmael away. What was left was the same situation they were in before, only now it was worse. Can you imagine Sarah's mood now? I am sure it was not a pleasant one.

Well, chapter 17 brings us to a very interesting conversation between Abraham and God. This is when God changed their names from Abram and Sarai to Abraham and Sarah. God also reiterates His promise of a son. Verse 2 says God will "multiply" Abraham "exceedingly." Verse 4 God says he will be a "father of a multitude of nations." Verse 6 God says he will be "exceedingly fruitful" and He will make "nations" of him. Verses 7-10 God makes reference to Abraham's "descendants."

Verse 16 God makes it extremely, notably, without-a-doubt plain that He will bless Sarah and "give you a son by her." Abraham then falls on his face, laughs in his heart and thinks to himself, "Will a child be born to a man one hundred years old? And will Sarah, who is ninety years old, bear a child?" (verse 17) He was forgetting just Who he was dealing with wasn't he? How often do we do the same, limiting God and putting Him in a box saying He can't do something?

It is interesting to note what Abraham says next, this time out loud to God. Verse 18, "Oh, that Ishmael might live before Thee!" – in other words, "Um, Lord, could you just follow the plan Sarah and I used? It would really make things a lot easier on everybody! I mean, Ishmael is already here and all." Sound familiar? How many times do we want God to cancel His perfect plans for our lives and do something else that we think would be better? And a lot of the times, it's only to get us out of the messes we get ourselves into!

I love God's reply. Without missing a beat, God again restates His promise. "Sarah thy wife shall bear thee a son indeed; and thou shalt call his name Isaac: and I will establish my covenant with him for an everlasting covenant, and with his seed after him." (Gen. 17:19 KJV)

Okay, now let's see what Sarah does when God directly gives her His promise. Chapter 18 tells the story of the three men who came to Sarah and Abraham. After the men have eaten what Abraham had prepared for them, one of them (the Lord) says, "I will certainly return unto thee according to the time of life; and, lo, Sarah thy wife shall have a son." (verse 10 KJV) Sarah was in the tent and heard what was said. She thought it was pretty funny seeing how old she and her husband were. She was way past the natural age for baring children. Verse 12 says she "laughed to herself."

The Lord replied, "Why did Sarah laugh, saying, 'Shall I indeed bear a child, when I am so old?'" Notice carefully what He said next: "Is anything too hard for the LORD? At the time appointed I will return unto thee, according to the time of life, and Sarah shall have a son." (Gen. 18:14 KJV)

In God's ordained time and not one millisecond sooner.

First of all, "with God all things are possible." (Matt. 19:26) Second, God said that He would return at the "appointed time." This "time" is not the nine months of pregnancy that Sarah would experience for He differentiates by saying "according to the time of life." So only in God's time did God fulfill Sarah's desire for a son. Isaac was born of Sarah and Abraham at the appointed, God ordained time and not one millisecond sooner.

Now apparently Sarah did believe what God said He would do, for she is in the Faith Hall of Fame – Hebrews 11:11. "Through faith also Sarah herself received strength to conceive seed, and was delivered of a child when she was past age, because she judged him faithful who had promised." (KJV) Sarah judged God faithful and true to His Word and once again God was just that. In the same way, we need to judge God faithful and true to His Word and will for our lives. No matter the situation, no matter what obstacles we think may be in the way, God comes out faithful every time. He is worthy of our trust. God is awesome all the time.

Over and over, God proves His success rate to be perfect and complete. There is nothing too big, nothing too small, and nothing too impossible for Him. God will fulfill His plan for our lives at the "appointed time." He knows what He's doing and He knows when, where and how to carry out all He has for us. We do have to be patient and wait on Him. Abraham was 75 years old when he left his home country and God said he would make of him a great nation. It was another twenty-five years until Isaac, God's promised son, was born. Things do not happen overnight. Things do not happen in our timing. Things happen in God's time – and that is truly the BEST time ever!

My friends, please do not underestimate God's success rate. He is trustworthy. He is faithful. His plan is perfect. And His timing precise. May we say along with David, "Thou hast dealt well with Thy servant, O LORD, according to Thy word." (Psalm 119:65) Indeed, "Let us hold fast the profession of our faith without wavering; (for he is faithful that promised;)." (Heb. 10:23, KJV)

God's work in our lives is nourishing, protective and comforting. It is a place where we can grow and develop in Him. "The LORD is good to all, And His tender mercies are over all His works." (Psa. 145:9 KJV) When I read this verse one night, I was so encouraged. I looked up the meaning of the word "mercies" and was shocked by what I found. Surely I had gotten the Hebrew numbers mixed up or something. *That* could not be what it meant! "Mercies" is the Hebrew word "racham" meaning, "#7356. compassion (in the plural.); by extensions the womb (as cherishing the foetus); by implication a maiden:--bowels, compassion, damsel, tender love, (great, tender) mercy, pity, womb." (Strong's Exhaustive Concordance of the Bible) I could see compassion, but a *womb*? What was that all about? But think about it for a minute. The womb is the place where a baby is nourished, protected from the world that would harm it and a place where it is comforted and secure while it grows and develops. Wow! God's work in my life is just such a place! When I am in His will and He is working in my life, I am nourished by my Abba Father, I am protected from the evil one and I am comforted by the God of all comfort!

So why would I want anything other than God's work in my life? Allowing God to carry out His plan in my life means allowing Him to do His perfect work in my life. It means me standing back out of the way so He has room to work.

Girls, don't let the devil spin you a line or plant those seeds of doubt in your mind. God's best IS the best. Contentment IS possible. Singleness IS a gift. God IS faithful. God's plan for your life IS awesome. And you ARE precious in His sight! "The LORD will perfect that which concerneth me; Thy mercy, O LORD, endureth forever; forsake not the works of Thine own hands." (Psa. 138:8 KJV)

Whatever God's plan for your life, whether it is a lifetime of singleness or a season of singleness and then marriage, accept the gift He bestows and glorify Him by putting it to His use. There is no better place to be than in His will. He knows what He's doing and it is AWESOME! Guaranteed!!! "Never measure God's unlimited power by your limited expectations." (*Our Daily Bread*, Vol. 48 Num. 11, February 20)

So my dear friends, be encouraged! You are not alone as you drive down the Single Lane. Not only is Jesus driving - and it's sure to be an adventure! - but there are many other non-married, unattached, awesome women who are traveling down this road right along with you! Let's make God the focus of our attention and serve Him with a passion! So put your sunglasses on, hop in your convertible, start singing His praises and drive with confidence through that wonderful and exciting life in the single lane!!! Hey…what can I say…

You've heard it straight from

the Old Maid's mouth!

☺ ☺ ☺